NAVIGATIO

EARLY VOYAGES IN THE NORTH PACIFIC

PETER CORNEY

This likeness of Peter Corney is an old photograph of a painting of Corney, which is now in the possession of Mr. Peter Breton of Brixham, South Devon, England. Mr. Peter Breton is a great-great-grandson of Peter Corney.

EARLY VOYAGES

IN THE

NORTH PACIFIC

1813≼1818

BY

PETER CORNEY

YE GALLEON PRESS

Fairfield, Washington

1965

Of this edition _____9/4_ copies were finished.

This is Copy Number _269_ .

PREFACE

Little is known of the life of Peter Corney other than what we may learn from reading his book. We know he left England in November, 1813, on the schooner *Columbia*, and that he made some eight visits to the Columbia river during the years 1814 to 1817. Peter Corney was the first mate of the *Columbia*, a vessel belonging to the North West Company. This ship sailed between Fort George (now Astoria) and California, Alaska, the Hawaiian Islands, and China. She sailed first under command of Captain Anthony Robson and later under a Captain Jennings. This schooner was sold in Hawaii in 1817. Corney lived in the Islands for several years before returning to England in February, 1820. It is sometimes assumed that Peter Corney remained in England from his return voyage of 1820 until the outward voyage of 1835‹36, however this is not correct for Corney was a seafaring man and he was on the Northwest Coast

7

in the autumn of 1830, and again in December of 1834, when his easy going methods ruffled the august dignity and Scotch blood of Chief Factor John Mc‹ Loughlin at Fort Vancouver – this when Corney nonchalantly appropriated a cask of brandy and a keg of bright varnish. He was at that time serving as an officer on board the HBC *Eagle*.

Corney spent most of the time from 1813 to 1835 in the employ of the North West Company, and later the Hudson's Bay Company, mostly as a ship's officer. We do not know the date or place of his birth but believe he was either English or Irish.

Peter Corney has over the years acquired a rep‹ utation as a pirate, an outgrowth of the fact that he took part in the raid on Monterey. This part of his career is cloudy but it does appear that romanticism has in this instance somewhat outdistanced reality. Weller states that the Monterey incident grew out of a commercial dispute with Spanish authorities who refused to allow British interests to establish a trading post at Monterey. The truth is more complex than that or one needs a broader view of early nineteenth century history. Spain was at that time rapidly losing her grip on possessions in the Western Hemisphere. The raging flames of sixteenth century conquest had long since burned to ashes. San Martin and Simon Bolivar were idealistic and successful revolutionaries in South America and Mexico was attempting to throw off the heavy yoke of Spain. Hypolite Bouchard was an Argentine patriot who wished to stir up the somewhat lethargic Spanish Californians. The raid on and partial burning of Monterey by a handful of English and Argentines showed the weakness of the Spanish government and in 1822 California swore allegiance to the Republic of Mexico and she remained a part of that country for 24 years until war between the United States and Mexico changed the political complexion of California. Monterey was chosen for Bouchard's strike because it was the capital of Spanish California. Whatever may have been Corney's reasons for assisting in the raid on Monterey we can be fairly certain that Bouchard's motives were patriotic and while the raid cannot be considered a resounding success it was at least humiliating to the Spanish authorities. Peter Corney was an experienced and competent ship's officer, not a young man at the time as he had spent five years sailing in the North Pacific and some years before that in the West Indies. Corney unquestionably commanded the *Santa Rosa* in the raid on Monterey and thereby acquired a reputation out of keeping with the picture we have of a handsome, respectable officer, a middle-aged man, husband to the lady-like Frances Loder.

We know that Peter Corney married Frances Loder in Cork, Ireland on May 2, 1820. As reports speak of Corney as 'an old man,' and as his wife survived him by nearly half a century, it reasonable to conclude that he married a girl younger than himself.

In July of 1835 he was again in England for on the 22nd. of that month he was appointed First Mate of the barque *Columbia*, built for the Hudson's Bay Company and used in this case as an escort for the little steam vessel, the *Beaver*, on her maiden voyage (and under sail) out to Fort Vancouver, half a world away.

Corney then made arrangements to bring his wife and four children out to Victoria on Vancouver Island. This was to be his last appointment, resulting in an unfinished voyage, for the log of the *Columbia* states that Peter Corney died on August 30, 1835, at which time "the ship was running down the English Channel, outward bound from Gravesend for Honolulu."

Thus ended the career of a colorful but little known sailing officer, born some time in the late 1700's, who spent his working life on shipboard in the early years of the 19th century. As far as our knowledge goes this was his only book. It is rare in the English printing and the historian, Hubert

Howe Bancroft, who worked extensively with North Pacific material, missed it completely.

Corney's book has some basic source material for Russian Alaska and Spanish California.

This material was first printed in the *London Literary Gazette* in 1821. It was printed for the second time, in Russian, in 1822*1823. It is very rare in the United States in the Russian printing, but copies exist in the Library of Congress and at Yale University. The Russian printing of Corney is not an exact translation of the London edition, as it is somewhat abridged and there are corrections and comments. The Russian version is listed on page 320 of Wickersham, *A Bibliography of Alaskan Literature, 1724*1924,* as follows: *No. 6151, Peter Corney. Puteshestvie G. P. Kornea k siev.*zapadynm beregam Ameriki i v Kitai v 1813*18, a prisovokupleniem izvies* tiia o Ross, poseleniakh na sem beregu Amereki.* (ie., Corney's voyage to the northwest coast of America and to China, with description of the Russian settle*

12

ments on that coast of America.) *Siev. Arkh. iii, 18;
iv, 19, 1822; iii iv, 1823.*

'Siev. Arkh,' is an abbreviation used for *Sievernyi
Arkhiv*, meaning 'Northern Archive,' and printed
in Russian.

The first two printings of Corney were in peri-
odical form but in 1896 Thomas Thrum published
the Corney narrative in book form, with a preface
by W. D. Alexander and under the title, *Voyages
in the Northern Pacific.* This third printing of Corney, in Honolulu, which at that date was still part of
the Kingdom of Hawaii, is now a scarce book but
should not be considered a rare item. It shows up
now and then in antiquarian book dealers' catalogs
and of course over the years at gradually increasing
prices. The Amtman catalog, Montreal, 1963, listed
a copy at 45 dollars. It may be noted that although
the Thrum edition was printed in book form some
of the copies were sold in the form of folded sheets
and unbound.

The Peter Corney narrative, still a little known book, is here published for the fourth time, and this time in the pleasant country village of Fairfield, Washington, which is 30 miles south of Spokane, and near the north margin of the Palouse farming district, scene of world record dry land wheat crops. This is a quiet farming village, 300 miles from tide water. We reflect also that this is 69 years after the Honolulu edition and 144 years after the first printing was done in London.

Fairfield, December, 1965   *Glen Adams*

IT IS A GOOD THING TO GIVE THANKS

We wish to thank . . .

Mrs. John Parris of Escondido, California, who fur-
nished a working copy of the book; Phoebe Harris,
History Department, Seattle Public Library; Mr.
Willard Ireland, Provincial Archives, in Victoria,
British Columbia; Dorothy Whitnah, Book Club
of California, San Francisco; Mrs. Joyce Haas, who
is Assistant Librarian, Hawaiian and Pacific Col-
lection, University of Hawaii, Honolulu; also Miss
Mary Johnson, Reference Librarian, Spokane Pub-
lic Library; Miss Ethel M. Solliday, City Librarian,
Monterey, California; Mary Avery (Mrs. Emmett
Avery), Archivist, Washington State University;
Pierre Brunet, Assistant Dominion Archivist, Pub-
lic Archives of Canada, Ottawa, Ontario; Anne
Jackson (Mrs. J. R. Jackson), also of Ottawa; the
University of Alaska, Fairbanks; Mr. Peter Breton,
of Brixham, South Devon, England; Mr. Archibald
Hanna, Western Americana Collection, Yale Uni-

versity, New Haven, Connecticut; Mr. Aleksis Rannit, Curator of Slavic Collections, Yale University; Mayo Hayes O'Donnell; the Reading Room of the British Museum, London, England; and the Hudson's Bay Record Society, also of London, which so graciously gave permission to quote the paragraphs from the *McLoughlin Letters, First Series, 1825‹38*; also Senor Horacio Baserga, San Carlos, California, who provided information on Hypolite Bouchard.

I wish also to thank Mr. E. W. Giesecke, Olympia, who furnished photostats of the J. Neilson Barry and Frederick W. Howay material.

THOMAS GEORGE THRUM

. . . . who published the 1896 edition of the Peter Corney narrative, was born at Newcastle, in South Wales, Australia, on May 27, 1842. His parents were Mr. and Mrs. Thomas Augustine Thrum. They had sailed from England a few years earlier to make a new life on a new continent.

Sea faring blood flowed in the veins of young Thomas G. Thrum, for his grandfather, one John Thrum, had sailed with Captain James Cook when that famed British explorer had discovered Hawaii in 1778. John Thrum later settled in Tahiti. In 1851 Thomas Augustine Thrum left Australia to live in Hawaii, and his family followed in 1852. The boy, Tom Thrum, made a leisurely trip of it, stopping off for a year in Tahiti to visit his grandfather. His keen young mind absorbed in that year all that his grandfather could tell him of the adventurous, col‹ orful days more than 70 years in the past, when as a teen aged boy he had sailed with Captain Cook.

In 1853 Tom Thrum, now eleven years old, was placed in the "Free School" for foreign children and there completed his formal education by the time he was fourteen. While still a schoolboy he had picked up a job clerking in the Honolulu store of John Thomas Waterhouse, and this led to another job boiling sugar on Kohala plantation. He then shipped on a whaler and later lived for a time in California.

Always with a good head for business he saved his money and in 1870, now aged 28, he married Miss Anna Laura Brown, an American girl residing in California. He then returned to Honolulu where he set himself up as an independent business man, a calligrapher, copyist, and a stencil plate cutter. Later that same year he expanded by buying a book store on Merchant street. Under able management the firm flourished and a branch store was opened on Fort street. The Merchant street site was later made a plant for bookbinding and printing and the Fort street business, selling books and stationery, became known as "Thrum's." The firm continued after Mr. Thrum's death and is now in the hands of a present day firm, the Honolulu Paper Company.

The bookbinding and printing business located on Merchant street was the scene of several publishing projects. Hawaii was at that time an independent kingdom and did not become a part of the United States until 1898. To publicize the kingdom of Hawaii and furnish information to local business men, Thrum published an annual handbook or almanac. When printing ink got deeper in his veins he tried publishing a weekly newspaper, a sheet called *The Islander*. This newspaper was launched in 1876 but it did not last long. The next publishing venture was started in 1881. This was *The Saturday Press*, and it fared better, lasting until

1886. For a short time there was still another pub‑
lication called *The Friend*. The most successful of
all the Thrum publications was a magazine, *The
Paradise of the Pacific*, which started in partnership
with J. J. Williams. This magazine is still published.

It is to Thrum's credit that he chose to retire
early from business at the age of 61, leaving business
affairs in the hands of his son. The rest of Thrum's
long life was spent in research on Hawaiian culture.
The crumbling ruins of the *heiaus*, or native stone
temples built before the coming of the white ex‑
plorers, were of intense interest to Thrum. He lo‑
cated and surveyed more than five‑hundred of the
old stone temples and collected a mass of legendary,
historical and factual material about the heiaus. The
result of this research was published in the Annual
over a period of several years. The publication of
this material encouraged other men to study the
heiaus so in later years the Bishop Museum took up
this work and further surveys of the native ruins

were made by Kenneth Emery and by Thomas F. G. Stokes, men who based their work on the earlier work of Thomas Thrum.

The deep interest Thrum had in the history and legends of Hawaii led him to master the written and spoken native Hawaiian language. This mastery of the native language led Thrum to appreciate the work of Abraham Fornander, who encouraged edu/cated Hawaiians to write the legends and literature of their people. At the time of Fornander's death he left untranslated a rich store of native manuscript material in the library of the Bishop Museum, and it was a logical step for the Museum trustees to hire Thomas Thrum to translate this material into the English language, which work was begun in 1915. While Thrum with some gentlemanly modesty nev/er signed his name to the work he translated for the Bishop Museum publications, or the Annual, other scholars have little difficulty recognizing his work. When he printed two volumes of his own he desig/

THE LONDON LITERARY GAZETTE,

AND

Journal of Belles Lettres, Arts, Sciences, &c.

This Journal is supplied Weekly, or Monthly, by the principal Booksellers and Newsmen throughout the Kingdom; but to those who may desire its *immediate* transmission, by post, we beg to recommend the LITERARY GAZETTE, printed on stamped paper, price One Shilling.

No. 237.   SATURDAY, AUGUST 4, 1821.   PRICE 8*d.*

Original.

VOYAGES IN THE NORTHERN PACIFIC, &c.&c.

WE announced a few weeks ago our intention of inserting in the LITERARY GAZETTE, when the season of issuing new and important publications had so far elapsed as to afford us room for other prominent articles besides Reviews, a succession of original papers, being the narrative of Voyages in the Pacific Ocean, and of other circumstances deeply interesting, not only to the curiosity and literature of Great Britain, but to its manufactures, commerce, and colonial prosperity. We now hasten to redeem our pledge, by laying before our readers the first Number of the promised Series, to be regularly continued, and to embrace the following subjects:—

Narrative of a Voyage from London to the Columbia River—An Account of the first Settlers thereon.

merce of the Northern Pacific, on all of which this MS. supplies very new and valuable notices. And the general question is so fairly handled in the writer's own preface, that we shall abstain from further comment, and allow him to state his own case, only observing that in addition to the preceding contents, there is a vocabulary of the language spoken on the north-west coast of America and Sandwich Islands, which may help to illustrate the labours of Captain Freycinet, announced by the French Savans.

PREFACE.

The only object of the author of this work is in making his observations on the trade between the north-west coast of America and the Sandwich Islands and China, is, to point out to the merchants of this country the vast trade that is carried on between those places by the Americans and the Russians while an English flag is rarely to be seen.

He would particularly wish to call the attention of the merchant of this country to the

1820, will show how far they are desirous of profiting by their possessions; "*Military Expedition to the Upper Missouri.*—The 6th regiment of infantry left Bell Fountain on the 4th October. Colonel Atkins commands the expedition. Thus the public have at length the satisfaction to see fairly embarked, this interesting expedition, on the security of which depends the accomplishment of such mighty objects of the American people—the transfer of the fur trade from the English to the Americans, the extinction of British influence among American Indians, and the opening a direct intercourse with India by the Columbia and Missouri rivers."

For several years past, it has been a favourite object of the American government to open an easy communication from their western settlements to the Pacific Ocean; and the above paragraph indicates the steps which have been taken to realize this vast project. The most western settlements which the Americans have are on the Missouri; and from the mouth of the Columbia on the Pacific Ocean, they are distant about 3,000

An Account of the present State of the Sandwich Islands.

And a Narrative of a Cruize in the Service of the Independents of South America in 1819.

The author of these pieces, which are written, in our opinion, with great simplicity and force of observation, is Peter Corney, mate of the schooner Columbia, of London, which vessel was sold to the King of the Sandwich Islands. He seems to have enjoyed, during the period of years he was in a quarter of the globe but very partially known to Europeans, peculiar opportunities for acquiring information, and to have availed himself of them in a manner worthy of a shrewd and intelligent man. He relates facts in a plain sailor-like style; and we shall be disappointed if his round unvarnished tale does not give as much satisfaction as the most elaborate work of any learned traveller. On the vital consequence of several of the subjects on which his observations turn, it is not necessary to say any thing—there is not a manufacturer nor merchant in England, who does not feel the importance of the North American fur trade, of the trade with China, and of the rising com-

selves, and cultivating an intercourse with other countries. The Russians are by no means ignorant of their importance, and have more than once attempted to obtain possession of them. To Russia they would be invaluable, as its colonists could cultivate sugar, tobacco, and coffee, and make rum sufficient for the supply of that vast empire. The effect which such a step would have on our West-India trade is too obvious to require any comment. However lightly the people of these islands may be thought of, there is an anxious wish on their part to cultivate intercourse with those who will trade with them, and there exists a desire for improvement beyond the most sanguine hope, of those who wish to see the condition of mankind bettered by social intercourse. Their battery or fort at Woahoo, where guard is mounted and relieved with as much regularity and form as at the Tower of London—the policy of the king in charging foreign vessels pilotage and harbour dues, because a brig that he had purchased from the Europeans and sent to China with sandal wood, had been made to pay pilotage and harbour dues, will prove that they are ready to imitate the customs of civilized nations.

The fur trade is now totally in the power of the Americans, as by the treaty of Ghent the establishment on the Columbia was given up to that republic. The following extract from the Montreal Herald of the 13th April;

the India, and the wild beasts of the forest range undisturbed, that offers such peculiar inducement to the American design—not of colonizing the country, though this consequence would undoubtedly follow; but of making an immediate inroad on barbarism, by establishing a chain of posts at the distance of 50 or 100 miles along the great rivers as far as the Pacific Ocean. The fur trade is the great object of attraction to settlers in this wilderness; and so lucrative is this traffic, that it is well calculated to excite a competition amongst rival states. It can only be prosecuted by such nations as have a ready access to these deserts, where the wild animals which afford this valuable article of trade multiply undisturbed by civilized man; and these nations are at present the British, whose possessions of Canada secures them access to the north-western deserts of America—the Americans, who have free access to the wilderness that lies between their territories and the Pacific Ocean; and the Russians, whose immense empire borders on the north-west coast of America, gives them ample opportunities, which they have duly improved, of establishing settlements on its shores—of cultivating a friendly intercourse with the natives, and of exchanging European articles for the valuable furs which they collect in the course of their hunting excursions. The fur trade has been prosecuted with amazing enterprize

This is the original *London Literary Gazette* printing of Corney, exact size nated himself as 'the compiler' rather than author. The reprinting of the Peter Corney narrative was of course just one of the many things that Thrum did for the history and literature of Hawaii.

In 1932 the University of Hawaii gave Thrum an honorary degree of Master of Arts, a high honor to be conferred upon a self educated man whose formal schooling had ended at the age of fourteen. Thrum lived to publish fifty-eight consecutive editions of the Annual and at his death left material on the islands for several more issues.

Thomas George Thrum, gentleman, business man, historian, scholar, and publisher, died in Honolulu on May 21, 1932, six days short of his ninety-first birthday.

Quoted from Earle V. Weller's Forward to *The Sack of California*, by Peter Corney, published in 1940 by The Book Club of California, its Keepsake Series *Pacific Adventures*, Number Four.

First published in the *London Literary Gazette* of 1821, the story of the sack of Monterey appeared in a small volume entitled *Voyages in the Northern Pacific* which was issued in Honolulu in 1896. The magazine articles escaped the notice of Bancroft, and the Hawaiian imprint is now a scarce item. It offers a first-hand account of early California under Spain, the first Russian settlements and relations between the Pacific Coast and the Hawaiian Islands. The author of the *Narrative*, Peter Corney, had served in the West India trade and, when a London expedition was organized in 1813 for exploration of the Northwest Coast of America, he was engaged as chief officer of the *Columbia*, a former American craft, under command of Captain Anthony Robson.

After a voyage marked by contrary winds and a mutiny which was only suppressed by the officers standing guard with loaded pistols day and night, the party reached the Columbia River, traded with the natives and Russians, landed the mutineers and proceded to the Hawaiian Islands. There they met King Kamehameha . . . (here Weller quotes a description of the King).

After a voyage to China, Robson turned the command of the *Columbia* over to Captain Jennings who returned to California and visited Monterey. Here is the picture Corney gives of the town in 1815 . . . (Weller quotes a page of description).

From Monterey Corney's party proceeded up the coast, anchored in Drake's bay and visited the the Russian settlement at Bodega. When the *Columbia* returned to Hawaii, Corney was offered the command of the *Santa Rosa*, a privateer. His first assignment, described in the final chapter of the *Narrative*, was the attack on the Spaniards who had refused to permit them to establish a trading post in Monterey.

On his return to England, Corney contributed the account of his experiences to the London magazine. A few years later he was appointed to an executive post with the Hudson's Bay Company in British Columbia. He reached Hawaii in 1836, embarked on his old ship, the *Columbia*, but died before the ship reached its destination.

Note: Corney probably died in 1835, rather than 1836, and Anne Jackson states that the *Columbia* of 1813 was a schooner owned by the North West Company and the *Columbia* of 1835 was a barque built for the Hudson's Bay Company, hence they appear to be two different vessels with the same name.

Here and there in old books can be found some reference to the elusive Peter Corney. He is said to be mentioned in an obscure book by Jacques Mac⸗ Carthy, *Choix de voyages dans les quatre parties du monde, ou Precis des voyages les plus interessantes par terre et par mer, entrepris depuis l'ann'ee 1806 jusqu'a ce jour*. Paris, Plassen, 1821⸗22. t. IX, p. 106.

The Peter Corney narrative would have been almost completely lost to the world if it had not been for the work of Thomas G. Thrum in locating and printing this in the Honolulu edition, in which state it is scarce but not rare.

Also in twentieth century books we can find a few words about Peter Corney. In ''Voyages to Hawaii Before 1860'' (Honolulu, 1929) p. 20, we find: *Columbia*, British registry, schooner, 185 tons, trader, Anthony Robeson, master; arrived January 16, 1815, departed January 18, 1815; Peter Corney, chief officer. The *Columbia* arrived again with her master given as Capt. Jennings, on December 10, 1815, and left on January 4, 1816. It is mentioned here that the *Columbia* had made three other visits. In 1817 we find the following entry: "*Columbia*, British registry, schooner, 185 tons, Capt. Jennings, master; arrived December 6, 1817; Peter Corney, chief officer; sold to Kamehameha I, May 2, 1818; (46). *Columbia* had made three previous visits. Also under the year 1818 we find an entry - *Santa Rosa*, "American built, about 300 tons." A pirate ship under Capt. Turner, she arrived in May of 1818; bought by Kamehameha I but seized by *Argentina*, Bouchard, late in September 1818; departed October 20, 1818 with Peter Corney in command; (46).

Then in 1940 the Book Club of California published a small item, one of their Keepsakes, *The Sack of California*, by Peter Corney, material taken from the Thrum edition, with a foreword by Earle V. Weller.

There is also a modern book on Peter Corney, *A Pirate Flag for Monterey*, written by Lester Del Rey, published in 1952. This is a story of the sack of Monterey, an account written for children and depicting Corney as a coarse, brutal pirate to some extent outwitted by a young boy. The story is complete with a pretty girl and obviously is fiction rather than history.

Little has been published in magazine form on Corney but we note one such item, "*Peter Corney's Voyages, 1814⁏1817*" by J. Neilson Barry, *The Oregon Historical Quarterly*, vol. 33, no. 4, p. 355⁏368, December, 1932.

For the curious minded who may wish to consider all facets there is a 1947 movie, *Pirates of Monterey*, with Maria Montez, Robert Cameron, and Gilbert Roland. The locale is right, the Spanish California period is right, and the idea of *pirates* rings a bell, but seeing the film leaves me baffled. There is a faint attempt at history, which takes an odd flavor as a critical viewer is astonished and amused when the pirates are politely termed 'royalists.' One is left with the impression that the story is fiction and that it wanders by accident in the direction of fact, or else that it pertains to some entirely different incident in California history. The names of Corney and Bouchard are not mentioned nor do the sea dogs get past the beach. One wonders how it might all seem to an impassive TV audience in 1965 had an attempt been made to show the blazing patri⁄otism of Hypolite Bouchard and the probable com⁄mercial motivation of Peter Corney,

A possible source of confusion is the circumstance that several ships engaged in the early North Pacific trade had the same name. Information on them is fragmentary and not in complete agreement, but a few facts may be helpful.

Columbia number one: or more properly, the *Columbia Rediviva,* out from Boston with Robert Gray as her master. She was a famous ship for Gray sailed her in his much publicized discovery of the Columbia river. She was a good sized ship for her day and was full rigged. Information on her can be found in an excellent book published by the Massachusetts Historical Society, 1941, Frederick William Howay, (1867-1943) *Voyages of the Columbia to the Northwest Coast, 1787ₜ1790 and 1790ₜ1793,* xxvii, 518 p. (Collections, v. 79.) The later years of this *Columbia* are something of a mystery. There are reports that the famous ship in a few years (after 1793) was worn out and taken to pieces, and soon her chief officers all passed away, however she lasted somewhat longer than such reports would indicate as her register in the National Archives was not cancelled until the fourteenth of October, 1801. Accompanying the cancellation is the laconic statement: *'ript to pieces.'*

Columbia number two: This is the ship on which Peter Corney sailed, 1813 to 1817, and of course is the vessel referred to in the Corney narrative. Rumors exist *Columbias one* and *two* are the same vessel although under different ownership and different national register. According to the ship register kept by Lloyd's of London, *Columbia number two* had been built in Baltimore, U.S.A. in 1812 and was of a sharp model - probably a Baltimore clipper schooner which, it would appear, had been captured during the war of 1812. (*Source: Marine Historical Associ-ation, Mystic, Connecticut.*) She was small, listed at 191 tons and bound for China. In 1819 her tonnage was increased to 207, indicating minor a alteration

33

in arrangement or that she had in some way been remeasured. We note that Peter Corney gives her register as 185 tons, and states that she carried a crew of twenty-five men including her officers, that she mounted ten 9 pound guns and was equipped with patent boarding defence all around her bulwark. In any case we can be certain that she was an altogether different vessel than *Columbia number one.* This second *Columbia* was sold to Kamehameha I on May 2, 1818. (*Source:* Adele Ogden, *California Sea Otter Trade, University of California Press, 1941.*) It is rumored that the ship was shortly afterward wrecked by her native crew.

Columbia number three: This was a barque of 309 tons, built in 1835 and registered to the Hudson's Bay Company, London. She was used for some years in the North Pacific trade. This is of course the ship on which Peter Corney died August 31, 1835, on her maiden voyage out to Oregon. Death came not far from the English shore and this date is confirmed by by an entry in the log of the *Beaver*, written in this fashion: *Log of the steamship* Beaver . . . *August 27, 1835* . . . *September 1* . . . *10 a.m., signal from the* Columbia, *wishing to speak to us. Hove to for her, and she reported the death of Mr. Carney* (sic), *her chief mate.*

There are occasional references to the *Columbia number three* in the records of the Hudson's Bay Company and in the *McLoughlin Letters.*The logs of other vessels mention her occasionally and now and then there is some word about her in the early United States government Congressional reports on the warm subject of the disputed Oregon country. We note one such mention in House Document No. 101, twenty-third Congress, 3rd. session, the Caleb Cushing report on the Territory of Oregon, dated February 16, 1839. We may detect a slight touch of envy here and a possible exaggeration of the value of the cargo as we quote a paragraph from page 30: (from the William A. Slacum Report)

"Early on the morning of the 24th, I crossed over in the boat to the fort, and found the ships alluded to by the Indians were the Hudson's Bay Company's ships *Nereide* and *Llama*, both loaded and ready for the sea; the former with the annual supply of goods suitable for the Indian trade at the Hudson's Bay Company's depots along the coast at the north, from Pugitt's sound, (*sic*) in latitude 47 deg. 30 min. north, to Fort Simpson, in 54 deg. 40 min. north; the latter with a valuable cargo of British manu⸗ factures, bound for St. Francisco, California. Ascertained the Hudson's Bay Company's ship *Columbia* crossed the bar on the 26th of November, bound to London, with a valuable cargo of furs and peltries, valued at £80,000 – $380,000.''

I do not have information on the final days of this vessel.

Columbia number four: There is a puzzling nebulous record on page 140 of the Frederick W. Howay, *A List of Trading Vessels in the Maritime Fur*

Trade, 1785 to 1825. We quote: "But in August, 1818, Roquefeiul met a brig *Columbia* near Hecate Strait. This brig was commanded by Robson, and had left Europe after the departure in 1817 of *l'Uranie* under Freycinet; but the *Columbia* of 1813 to 1817 was delivered to *King Kamehameha* on May 2, 1818. If the dates are correct this is plainly a different vessel. Nothing further has been ascer‹ tained.

It is not impossible that other early vessels in the North Pacific trade also were named *Columbia,* but these four are the sailing ships which have come to the attention of historians.

The name of Father Davis, History Department, Gonzaga University, Spokane, was inadvertently omitted from the list of individuals who provided bits and pteces of information on Peter Corney. Father Davis provided information on the several *Columbias.*

FRANCES LODER CORNEY

This is a photograph of an oil painting of Frances Loder, married to Peter Corney. She was born around the year 1800 and died January 23, 1874. The painting is owned by Mr. Peter Breton, Brixham, England, a great-great-grandson of Peter Corney and his wife.

ANNE CORNEY DUDOIT

This is the beautiful Anne Corney who on January 8,
1837, at the tender age of 15 years and 9 months, married
Jules Dudoit, French Consul for Hawaii, and who over
the years mothered ten children.

The Archivist of the Hudson's Bay Company tells us that Peter Corney offered his services as the second officer on the Company's brig, the *Eagle*, in 1829, and subsequently served in that capacity, and was afterwards Chief Mate aboard the *Columbia* (also belonging to the company) in 1835. There is a possible minor error in W. D. Alexander's introduction to the 1896 edition in regards to Corney's death. Alexander gives this as 1836, where the Library of the British Museum, and the Hudson's Bay Company state that Peter Corney died on the 31st of August, 1835. The ship was at that time running down the English Channel, outward bound from Gravesend for Honolulu. The log goes on record that the body of the deceased was committed to the deep the next day. This information was taken from the log of the *Columbia* and any interested reader is referred to the Hudson's Bay Company Archives, HBC. C1/243, Fol. 3rd. and 4. Thus death came not far from the English coast and many thousands of miles from his beloved Hawaii.

The following references are taken from the Hud؛ son's Bay Record Society publication *McLoughlin Letters, First Series, 1825؛38:*

Captain Aemiliius Simpson's report to McLoughlin of "his voyage to Nass," written aboard the *Cad؛ boro,* September 23, 1830. (p. 308)

"On the 29th August 1830 the *Cadboro's* & *Eagle's* boats were dispatched under Messrs. Sinclair & Corney to sound the channel a few miles beyond our anchorage (in the outer harbor of Nass) . . ." (*Note:* St. Nass is a river north of the *Skeena* and south of the *Stikene,* and was in the area served by Fort Simpson.)

McLoughlin to the Governor and Committee, November 18, 1834 (p. 130)

"Mr. Corney two days ago applied to me for leave to bring his wife and children to this country and told me that he had applied to your honors and that you had referred him to me."

Footnote 2. A.1/59, fos. 69d.*70, at a committee,

July 22, 1835, "Resolved that Mr. Peter Corney be appointed Chief Mate of the Barque *Columbia* and that he be allowed to take his wife and his four children out in the vessel to remain in the Country; his wife to mess with him at the Captain's table, the children in the steerage and that he be charged at and after the rate for three persons say *4s. 6d.* per diem for the whole, further that they be no expence to the Company for their maintenance in the Coun⟨ try, it being understood that the Chief Factor in charge may engage Mrs. Corney in any capacity, for the education of the Natives or any other that she may be qualified for."

McLoughlin to the Governor and Committee, March 14, 1835. (p. 136)

"Since the departure of the *Eagle* I was informed that Mr. Handley who came in her had told Capt. McNeill, that Mr. Corney had tapped a Keg of bright Varnish, part of the cargo of the *Eagle* consigned to this place. I enquired of him if it was so, and he tole (*sic*) me it was so, that he had done it himself by order of Mr. Corney. I requested him to give me a statement of this in writing, which he refused and I immediately put him off duty; this occurred 10th December 1834. It was not the value of the Varnish (though the half of it was taken and we have not what we require for the Vessels here) but as your Honors will perceive what makes me so particular in this instance is to prevent any other in the future committing such an impropriety as tapping any Barrels belonging to the Cargo. A cask of Brandy for this place was expended on board the *Eagle*, the excuse given by Mr. Corney was that he thought it was part of the Ship's stores, and I said no more about it. But you see by the accounts gone home charged it to the *Eagle*.

The Hawaiian Historical Society has courteously made available the contents of a note written in the handwriting of Mr. W. D. Alexander (author of the 1896 Thrum preface), which states: "*Peter Corney, Sen., embarked for the Islands in 1834* (sic) *with his wife, and 4 children; viz, Peter, Fanny, Emily, & Anna. The old man died on the voyage. An old chief, "Old Snuff," and his wife, Puluna, took in his family, near site of Masonic Blding. Peter Jr. was a carpenter. Anna married Dudoit in 1836. Emily died of consump‹ tion."*

Note: The date of 1834 in Alexander's hand writing is almost certainly an error for 1835. Emily may in‹ deed have died of consumption but she did not die until 1870 or 1871, at which time she would have been 36 or 37 years of age.

It should be noted that Corney records his version of the latitude and longitude of the wreck of the *Tonquin*, captured by the natives about the middle of June, 1811, and blown up by a seriously wounded member of her crew. It is believed that the natives killed all aboard her except the interpreter, who was himself a native and member of a tribe farther south. Corney apparently observed the wreckage personally and not many months after the destruc∗ tion of the vessel. He gives us a location that comes close to Queenex Rocks, Nasparti Inlet, on the south edge of Cape Cook or Brooks Peninsula, Vancouver Island. This is the only known narrative to give an exact reference to a possible location for the wreck of the *Tonquin*. Bancroft locates the *Tonquin* in less exact terms, as *opposite a village on the bay of Clayo∗ quot, near the entrance of the Strait of Fuca*.

This is an enlarged view of an impression taken in sealing wax of Peter Corney's personal seal. In the box where this is kept there is a tiny illustration showing the St. George's cross in red and all other detail in black on a white background. The birds are believed to be doves, this from the tufts of feathers on their heads. Birds are often used on English seals and standards, including the standard of the Duke of Edinburgh. This photograph was furnished by Mr Peter Breton, a great-great-grand-son of Peter Corney.

HYPOLITE BOUCHARD

One of the many courageous and colorful men who helped weave the fabric of Latin America was Hypolite Bouchard. Captain Bouchard was French, born near Marseilles, France, in the latter part of the eighteenth century, but brought to Buenos Aires at an early age, grew up in the New World to be a a dedicated Argentine patriot.

Bouchard was intimately involved in the revo/ lutionary birth pains of Argentina, taking part in the bloody land fighting, and in 1810 was given command of some ships of the newly formed Arg/ tine Republic. Later and once more on land he fought alongside Gral. Don Jose de San Martin. On the shores of Parana he captured an enemy flag in a cavalry charge. His courage in this campaign prompted the Argentine government to grant him honorary citizenship on April 29, 1813. His marriage to a distinguished Argentine lady and the birth of two daughters further cemented bonds with his adopted country.

After a number of naval engagements fought on the coasts of Argentina and Chile, Bouchard sailed deep Pacific waters in command of the frigate *La Argentina* under the blue and white flag of the new nation, proclaimed free of Spanish rule on July 9, 1816. He sailed as a privateer under orders from San Martin to harrass Spanish shipping. By defin﹣ ition a privateer is an armed private vessel that is commissioned to cruise against the commercial ves﹣ sels or warships of the enemy.

Bouchard's objective was to undermine the fal﹣ tering Spanish naval system, particularly in the Philippines, and to encourage insurrections along those American shores still dominated by Spain. As we review dispassionately today the scope of this objective the fact that the cruise was not completely successful becomes understandable.

A great deal of ocean water was covered in this

cruise. Outside the port of Tamatava in the island of Madagascar Bouchard surprised four English and French vessels loading slaves, an illegal occupation. In righteous anger Bouchard held these four ships at bay for ten days until the British corvette *Combay* came to relieve him.

Then after an epidemic killed most of his crew Bouchard had a dangerous encounter with Malay pirates. Outnumbered and blessed with a remark⸴ ably windless day, which deprived him of much use of his sails, there was no alternative to a bloody hand to hand battle. The Malays surrounded the ship and attempted to board *La Argentina* when her guns roared out and this superior fire power wrecked several of the pirate junks. In the hand to hand fighting that followed a number of Malays were captured and the resourceful Bouchard impressed some twenty of the best into service on his own ship to replace the forty men he had just lost in the epidemic.

Sailing northeastward with a reduced and sick‑ened crew Bouchard arrived in Hawaii where he found another Argentine vessel, the *Santa Rosa*, sometimes known as the *Cacabuso*. Her crew had mutinied and had operated the vessel as a pirate ship, but tiring of this hazardous occupation, or charmed by Hawaii or the native Hawaiian girls, they sold the *Santa Rosa* to King Kamehameha for two casks of rum and 600 quintals of sandal‑wood, a transaction that did not please Captain Bouchard. Meanwhile the mutineers had scampered inland, taking refuge on the island of Atoy where an inde‑pendent king had given them asylum. When the king refused to turn in the mutineers Bouchard added the quiet persuasion of *La Argentina's* cannon and the men were immediately turned over. With some disapproval of the previous behavior of the mutineers Bouchard stood them up on the beach and shot them.

Bouchard then repossessed the *Santa Rosa*, and

recruited a native crew, also an English sailing offi‹ cer, Peter Corney. And for thoughtful armchair historians who may not completely understand early nineteenth century military procedures, we include the information that Bouchard carefully recruited thirty young Hawaiian women to ease the hardships of the voyage. (*Source: Mayo Hayes O'Donnell and the Monterey Peninsula Herald.*)

On October 25, 1818, the *Santa Rosa*, and *La Argentina* set sail for Alta California with no less an objective than the overthrow of Spanish rule in that province. Sailing a northeast course the expedition raised land three weeks later and Bouchard paid a discreet visit to Kusof, commander at Fort Ross, the Russian settlement on Bodega Bay, to learn what he could of the political situation in Alta California, and to purchase supplies for his men. Beef and wheat were scarce at Fort Ross but supplies of fish, venison and bear meat were obtained and the ships sailed south, entering Monterey Bay on November

22nd. The plan was to send the *Santa Rosa* to rec⸍ onnoiter any fortified works and to make a landing from her under cover of darkness. Weather con⸍ ditions were unfortunate, a dead calm descended and strong currents caused the ships to drift apart.

La Argentina had to anchor two miles offshore, while the *Santa Rosa* after considerable maneuvering in the gathering fog succeeded in entering the har⸍ bor where she anchored off an unidentified head⸍ land dimly seen through the mist. During the night men were silently transferred from *La Argentina* to the *Santa Rosa*, a long and tedious process as the men were weak. At dawn Bouchard was dismayed to find that the *Santa Rosa* had anchored within easy range of two batteries of shore artillery, and a battle followed which the Spanish should have won easily but which it appears they managed to lose rather easily. When the Argentine forces were landed they found that the Spanish Californians had already executed the technical maneuver known as getting the hell out of there. The accounts of the landing are fragmentary and contradictory but there is some evidence that the Argentines came ashore firing steadily but with powder only, no bullets. Certainly a minimum amount of damage was done to the local citizenry and we must remember that it was Bou⸗ chard's objective to arouse the lethargic Californians to revolt against the Spanish Crown, and to unite with Mexico where bloody fighting was already taking place.

The flag of Argentina was flown over the Presidio at Monterey supposedly for five days following the landing. Clearly it was Bouchard's intention to arouse the spirit of freedom in the people and to win them over to his cause, the liberty of America. Unfortunately the outcome was not just what he expected, the somewhat lethargic Californians con⸗ tinued to be somewhat lethargic and Bouchard was unable to overcome their indifference or to involve them emotionally with the troubles in Mexico.

Failing in this he decided to destroy the garrison and Spanish government stores, simply as a military measure. Under his orders the Spanish and major part of Monterey was burned. It is an established fact that Bouchard had orders to destroy only such property as was Spanish and the homes of native Americans were carefully preserved.

Seven days after their arrival the two vessels left Monterey and following this raided again and with indifferent success at Mission San Juan Capistrano where they got little than fresh beef. In some way six of Bouchard's men were left ashore in the second raid; one of them, Joseph Chapman, of Boston, was possibly the first United States citizen to become a permanent resident of Spanish California, although the point is not clear and there were in California at that date a few men of uncertain origin who were considered to be *Americanos*.

Aboard his flagship Bouchard must have stared at the disappearing shores in disbelief that these Spanish Californians had not chosen Liberty when its hand had been offered, and at no more price than to live and die for it, as men of courage were doing elsewhere in the brave New World.

On the homeward voyage and apparently without much assistance from Peter Corney, Bouchard raided on the west coast of Mexico, again with indifferent success. Following the disbanding of the Argentine navy he served as a commander in the Peruvian navy, but from then on his career is uncertain. It is rumored that he was murdered on a trading expedition in the interior.

We have little way of knowing today exactly why the gentlemanly Peter Corney joined forces with the Argentine patriot, Hypolite Bouchard, in an expedition that failed. Any effort we may make in this direction is pure conjecture. It is evident that Sr. Bouchard had ability and a full share of Latin courage and about him there might well have been some personal magnetism. And what if this audacious plan had succeeded? Captain Bouchard, skilled at land fighting as well as on a quarterdeck, might have risen as the leader of a revolt against Spanish rule in Alta California, and by his side there might have been an English officer, Peter Corney, intent on opening California to British trade, and possibly to British immigration - recalling that at this date there were only a handful of U.S. citizens in California and very few in the inland Pacific Northwest, although the 'Boston' men had in the British view taken much more than their fair share of the maritime fur trade. The stakes were high in this game. It is easy to say that Bouchard and Corney tossed and lost - but did they lose in the end? The raid on Monterey unquestionably showed up the weakness of Spanish rule in Alta California, and in less than four years California, realizing the hopelessness of the Spanish position, swore allegiance to the Republic of Mexico. Peter Corney and Hypolite Bouchard may have accomplished more than they understood on that day in late November of 1818 when they so regretfully bore out to sea from the Alta California shore.

THE ANNE JACKSON LETTER

A number of descendents of Peter Corney are now living in Hawaii, British Columbia, Alberta, Ontario, England, and South Africa. Living in a modern world today not all of them would be interested in their color; ful, sea; faring ancestor, but we received an historically valuable letter from one Anne Jackson of Ottawa, who is a great; great; granddaughter of Peter Corney.

June 11, 1965

Dear Mr. Adams,

Thank you for your letter of June 8th. You have put some doubts in my mind about the date of Peter Corney's death. It is extremely difficult to learn very much about him so I would be most grateful if you would let me have any information you have.

My cousin, Mrs. Penno, the former Colleen Breton, has the family Bible in Dartmouth, Eng; land. Two or three years ago I was in England

staying with Colleen and I copied down the infor‹
mation from the Bible. It was given to Frances
Corney by Mr. A. Judd on November 11, 1847, and
by her to her grand‹daughter, my grandmother,
Mrs. Alice Maude Dudoit. Alice Maude was Jules
Dudoit's youngest child. All his children were
Christened in the Roman Catholic church or Cath‹
edral in Honolulu but Alice was a small child when
her father was killed and presumably that is why
she was confirmed an Anglican in Honolulu, and
presumably that is why the Bretons have the Corney
Bible and not the Dudoits.

According to the family Bible: Frances Loder
married Peter Corney in Cork, Ireland, May 2nd,
1820. Unfortunately neither of the births are re‹
corded in the Bible.

Frances Corney died Jan. 23rd, 1874.

Peter Corney died at sea, August 30th, 1836.

Loder is a name well known in racing circles in
Dublin. I found the Loders listed in the telephone

book in Cork and wrote to a name listed in Dublin hoping to learn something about Frances Corney, but there was no reply.

The *Columbia* on which Corney died traveled with the steamer *Beaver*. I find I have copied notes down out of a book in the Archives that the *Beaver* and the *Columbia* reached Fort George on the Co‹ lumbia River April 4th 1836. Since ships usually went to the Sandwich Islands first there seems to be something wrong, either with the date of Corney's August 30th death or with the *Columbia's* April 4th arrival at Fort George. Since Peter was going to Victoria it seems unlikely that he would have gone back to the Hawaiian Islands after reaching Fort George.

It took six or eight months to sail from England to the Pacific so the *Columbia* might well have left England in 1835 and reached the Sandwich Islands in 1836. According to family tales Corney died near the Islands. Had he died in the English channel it is unlikely that his wife and four children would have been taken to the Pacific.

Peter and Frances had four children:

Anne Corney, born April 28, 1821, christened at Lambeth Palace, London, England. According to the Hawaiian records she was christened *Ann* and confirmed *Anne*. Anna was probably a nickname.

Peter Minors Corney, born July 21, 1824, and who was christened at Stephen Church, London, Eng-land. We do not know if Peter married or not. He died in Honolulu, November 5, 1876.

Sarah Frances Corney, born February 26, 1826, and christened at Stephen Church, London, England. She died about 1901.

Emily Handley Foster Corney, born June 14, 1834, christened at Stephny (Stephen?) Church, London, England. She died June 23, 1870 (it may be 1871,) at Oakland, California.

At one time . . . I would *guess* from 1821 to 1834, Peter Corney lived at 7, Mount Street, Walworth, England.

Anne Corney married Jules Dudoit in Honolulu January 8, 1837. He was a good deal older than his wife. According to my records they had ten children. Jules was born in 1839 and the youngest, Alice Maude, (my grandmother,)was born in 1857.

Anne was an Anglican but as far as I know only her youngest child grew up to be an Anglican and she married a Methodist but I think we are all Anglicans. I say "I think" because our Irish relatives go to the Weslyn Church.

Alice Maude Dudoit married William Edwards Breton in Cork, Ireland, on March 11, 1880. Maude and Willie are buried in Langrish Parish Church in England. The record reads as follows: *William Edwards Breton, Inspector General, R.N., Born July 15, 1850; Died June 5, 1914. Alice Maude Breton, Born August, 1857, Died August 31, 1935.*

They had five sons. The two oldest, Kenneth and Guy, joined the Royal Navy, reaching the rank of

Captain, (surgeon Captain and engineer Captain.) The three younger boys started out homesteading in Alberta, just what one would expect of three great grandsons of Peter Corney!

My father, Basil Breton, is the youngest of the five sons of Willie and Maude Breton. Having lived hither and yon as a boy he came to Canada at the age of 17, joining two brothers and a Breton cousin. My grandparents also spent a short time in Alberta and my grandmother returned many more times before she died.

Basil Breton joined the Canadian Army in World War I and from England went to India to the Indian Army and stayed there until the end of the war in that part of the world. From the twenties until 1938 he lived on Vancouver Island. Then he went to Antigua to start the first tourist hotel in Antigua. He managed the Antigua Beach Hotel for ten years. Then he became the first executive secretary of the newly formed Industrial Development Board, and during the Second World War he was liaison officer between the British and American forces; surely a suitable role for a man who became a Canadian at the age of seventeen! For ten years he was the Com‚ munity Players director. The Community Players are assorted shades from coffee to black black with various white people helping from time to time. My father has written a manuscript of his twenty‚five years in Antigua and in this he shows some of his great grandfather's pioneering spirit.

To go back to your letter: The family Bible gives August 30, 1836 for Peter Corney's death. Since the *Columbia* sailed with the steamer *Beaver* it may be possible to check the dates through the *Beaver*.

The *Columbia* of 1813 to 1818 is not the same as the *Columbia* of 1836. The first was a schooner con‚ nected with the Northwest Fur Company and the second was a barque and was built by the Hudson's Bay Company.

We do not know Peter Corney's date or place of

birth, nor do we know whether he was English or Irish. Since Loder is a well known name in Ireland it is likely that Frances Loder, Peter's wife, was Irish. Bantry Bay was an English port so it is quite likely that Corney traveled to Cork or Bantry Bay when he was on the west Indian part of his career. Possibly if one could search church records in Cork or in Bantry Bay one might find some trace of the name Corney, which I have been told is an Irish name.

The family churches are confusing. Peter Corney married Frances Loder in Christ Church, an Anglican church in Cork in 1820. This Church is still in use and I saw the book in which their names are registered. (I was told that a member of the crew of the *Bounty* was a member of the congregation but unfortunately, being in a hurry with little time to learn about my own family, I neglected to write down the name of the man.)

Ann Corney must have been an Anglican, but since her children were christened in the Catholic

church or Cathedral, built at a later date, her hus‹
band, Jules Dudoit, must have been a Catholic.

Alice Maude Dudoit, who was my grandmother,
was christened in the R.C. cathedral and confirmed
in the Anglican church in Honolulu.

Maude Dudoit, youngest child of Anne and Jules
Dudoit, married William Edwards Breton, a Meth‹
odist, in St. Paul's *Anglican* church in Cork. Willy
Breton was born in Cork. St. Paul's, Christ Church
and an old Huguenot church, to which the Bretons
may have belonged, (church records were burnt,)
are all within easy walking distance of each other.
St. Paul's and the Huguenot church are now ware‹
houses for grocers.

Corney's *Breton* descendants are, as far as I know,
all *Anglicans* but, unless any of Maude Dudoit's
brothers or sisters became Anglicans, the other de‹
scendants are probably all Roman Catholics.

Maude Dudoit's third son was Douglas Corney
Breton, who was an M.P. in Alberta, and a small

village was named *Breton* after him.

If by any chance your study of Pacific Northwest history includes any mention of the brig schooner *Clementine*, or HBM *Opal*, I would appreciate receiving information about them. I am trying to put the family history together and those two ships were on the Pacific coast.

To sum up the church affiliations:

Peter and Frances ⸓ *Anglican*.

Maude Dudoit ⸓ *Roman Catholic* then *Anglican*.

William Breton ⸓ *Methodist*.

Breton children; Kenneth, Douglas, Lawerence, Guy, and Basil ⸓ all *Anglican*.

Sincerely,

Anne Jackson,

(Mrs. J. R. Jackson)

(*Note:* It is observed that the date of Peter Corney's death as given in the family Bible does not agree with the log of the *Columbia*, but we reflect that the log entry was a contemporary record where in this case the Bible record was not made until 1847, or later.)

THE PETER BRETON LETTER

Mr. Glen C. Adams
Postmaster
Fairfield
Washington
U.S.A.

Verbena
Milton Street
Brixham
South Devon
England

5th August 1965

Dear Mr. Adams,

I was very interested and pleased to receive your letter this morning, especially since I heard that someone was about to reprint my great-great grand-father's book and I was hoping to obtain a copy.

I live in the fishing port and holiday resort of Brixham where one can keep a yacht and get to sea in any spare time available, that as you have evi-dently heard is my chief hobby. I have a Real Estate business in the small town of Totnes some ten miles inland where I am also a member of our Rotary Club.

So far as Peter Corney is concerned I do not suppose I can give you any information other than that which my cousin Ann Jackson has supplied. She is the most efficient historian in the family and when she was over here went very thoroughly through any papers which we had, including the family Bible, with the date of his marriage, etc. in it. My sister, Colleen Penno, who lives at Dartmouth, quite near to us has the Bible and I spoke to her on the phone this morning to verify certain facts.

We know that Peter Corney was married in Cork, Ireland in 1820 to Frances Loder. I visited the Church in Cork where they were married when I was over there a little while ago and also asked those members of the family who are still there if they could recall either the names Corney or Loder and although my father's cousin, Mrs. Sarah McCann has lived there all her life she does not think that either name is Irish. She is well over eighty.

We also have a very fine china loving cup, now

lodged in the Plymouth Museum and always known as the Corney Cup. This has hand painted scenes of Oxford on it which may be some indication of where Peter Corney originally came from. The cup was probably a wedding present.

I have a portrait of Peter Corney, also portraits of his wife, Frances, and his daughter, Ann, who was born in Lambeth, London, in 1821; also a por≠ trait of a lady known as Mrs. Handley. Since one of his daughters became a Mrs. Emily Handley Foster I think this must be her portrait. I obtained photographs of the portraits of Peter, Frances, and Ann, which I sent to my cousin and these I think you have.

All of Corney's children were born in Lambeth, and Peter Corney is recorded as having died at sea. We presume his connections with Cork and Lam≠ beth were mainly maritime, since there does not seem to be any other particular reason why he should have been in either place.

Amongst other interesting bits and pieces my sister Colleen has Corney's signet ring and a copy of the 1896 edition of his book. I have the imprint of his seal and a colored copy. This was a St.Georges cross with three choughs or some other kind of black bird in the quarters with his initials P. C. in Gothic capitals underneath.

In his portrait Corney looks to be a highly respectable gentleman and I doubt that he would have been accepted into the then fashionable Prot‹estant church in Cork if he had not at least been considered respectable. At sea he was possibly a grimmer character although I would describe him as a successful privateer. I have a book published in Philadelphia, called *A Pirate Flag for Monterey*, by Del Ray. It is a childrens book but describes Corney as the most fearful pirate so he may have been a little ruthless up and down the coast, assum‹ing that the author must have gotten the idea from somewhere.

His daughter Ann married a man named Dudoit who I think was the French consul in Honolulu and was subsequently murdered by his Chinese cook. Their daughter married my grandfather who was a surgeon in the Navy. Grandfather was certainly brought up in Cork and we know that my grand mother was also there before she married, so the the Corneys must have had some connection with Cork. It is peculiar, although of no bearing on the Corney story, that my grandfather Breton was born in Cork, married Alice Dudoit and he then was stationed in Honolulu and at this same time my grandparents on my mother's side called Walker were also living in Honolulu, with their children, altogether a strong connection with the Pacific.

I rather think I have rambled on for a longish time on this matter. Peter Corney has always fas cinated me especially since I first went to Cork and dug about some two years ago. Practically all the male members of the family since Peter Corney have served at sea in the Navy, including myself, and if not they have never been able to stay at home for long, being inveterate globe trotters - it is rather a pity that we cannot find any actual descendents or antecedents with the name of Corney. My Uncle Basil Breton, Ann Jackson's father, recently went back to Honolulu and he reckons that there are quite a few relations there of Corney descent born on the wrong side of the blanket. There is I believe some truth in this although he has a vivid imagination, especially as far as Peter Corney is concerned whom he has always described as a pirate.

Yours sincerely,
Peter Guy Duperre Breton.

P.S. These are all family names, Peter from Corney and Guy Duperre from a French Admiral who was Alice Dudoit's husband's Uncle. He I think was also born at sea under odd circumstances.

EARLY VOYAGES IN THE NORTH PACIFIC

Voyages iŋ the Northern Pacific.

NARRATIVE OF SEVERAL TRADING VOY-
AGES FROM 1813 TO 1818, BETWEEN
THE NORTHWEST COAST OF AMERICA,
THE HAWAIIAN ISLANDS AND CHINA,
WITH A DESCRIPTION OF THE RUSSIAN
ESTABLISHMENTS ON THE NORTH-
WEST COAST.

INTERESTING EARLY ACCOUNT OF KAME-
HAMEHA'S REALM; MANNERS AND
CUSTOMS OF THE PEOPLE, ETC.

AND SKETCH OF A CRUISE IN THE SERVICE OF THE
INDEPENDENTS OF SOUTH AMERICA IN 1819, BY

PETER CORNEY.

WITH PREFACE AND APPENDIX OF VALUABLE CON-
FIRMATORY LETTERS PREPARED BY

PROF. W. D. ALEXANDER.

THOS. G. THRUM, PUBLISHER.
HONOLULU, H. I.
1896.

75

Reprinted from *The London Literary Gazette* of 1821.

PREFACE.

The following narrative by Mr. Peter Corney is now published in a separate form for the first time. As may be seen, it was first published serially in a weekly literary magazine in London, during the year 1821.

It seems to have been entirely over looked by the historians of the North-west Coast of America as well as by those of the Hawaiian Islands. It even escaped the researches of the indefatigable H. H. Bancroft and of Robt. Greenhow, the historian of Oregon.

The author was once well known in Honolulu, and has a number of descendants living here. He died in 1836, on board of the bark *Columbia*, while on his way to what is now called British Columbia, where he was to occupy a responsible position in the service of the Hudson's Bay Company. In consequence of his death his wife and children decided to remain in Honolulu, instead of continuing their voyage to the North-west Coast.

His narrative is a valuable contribution to the history not only of the North-west Coast, but also of the Hawaiian Islands. In particular, it throws much light on the proceedings of the

Russians here in 1815—1817, on the mutiny and piracy of the crew of the Argentine cruiser, *Santa Rosa*, her recapture by Capt. Bouchard of the frigate *Argentina*, and their homeward voyage, including the sack and burning of Monterey, California. It is also valuable as containing an account by a fair-minded eye-witness of the state of things in the islands near the close of Kamehameha's reign, which confirms the statements made by Alexander Campbell, James Hunnewell and other early visitors and residents.

W. D. ALEXANDER.

Honolulu, April, 1896.

CONTENTS

———◆◆◆———

INTRODUCTORY.

CHAPTER I.

CHAPTER II.

CHAPTER III.

CHAPTER IV.

CHAPTER V.

CONTENTS.

CHAPTER XII.

CHAPTER XIII.

CHAPTER XIV.

CHAPTER XV.

EARLY

VOYAGES.

INTRODUCTORY.

Observations on importance of N. W., Sandwich Islands and China trade.—Russian designs for control. —Rapid civilization of Sandwich Islanders.—They desire intercourse with foreign traders.—Customs of other nations readily adopted.—Fur trade in hands of Americans.—Likely extinction of British influence therein.—Opening up of Western country through to the Pacific.--Lewis and Clark's journey across the Rocky Mountains.—Variety of fur bearing animals observed.—Plans of Americans to form settlements; establish a town at the mouth of the Columbia River and found colonies on the Pacific Ocean shore.—Rapid growth of their population assures this.

THE only object the author of this work has in making his observations on the trade between the north-west coast of America and the Sandwich Islands and China, is, to point out to the merchants of this country the vast trade that is carried on between those places by the Americans and the Russians while an English flag is rarely to be seen.

He would particularly wish to call the attention of the people of this country to the state of the Sandwich Islands, by pointing out their vast importance to the West-India merchants; also the rapid progress the natives are making towards civilization (unaided by missionaries) by improving themselves, and cultivating an intercourse with other countries. The Russians are by no means ignorant of their importance, and have more than once attempted to obtain possession of them. To Russia they would be invaluable, as its colonists could cultivate sugar, tobacco, and coffee, and make rum sufficient for the supply of that vast empire. The effect which such a step would have on our West-India trade is too obvious to require any comment. However lightly the people of those islands may be thought of, there is an anxious wish on their part to cultivate intercourse with those who will trade with them, and there exists a desire for improvement beyond the most sanguine hope, of those who wish to see the condition of mankind bettered by social intercourse. Their battery or fort at Woahoo (Oahu), where guard is mounted and relieved with as much regularity and form as at the Tower of London; the policy of the king in charging foreign vessels pilotage and harbor dues, because a brig that he had purchased from the Europeans and sent to China with sandal wood had been made to pay pilotage and harbor dues, will prove that they are ready to imitate the customs of civilized nations.

The fur trade is now totally in the power of the Americans, as by the treaty of Ghent the establishment on the Columbia was given up to that republic. The following extract from the Montreal Herald of the 18th April, 1820, will show

how far they are desirous of profiting by their possessions: *"Military Expedition to the Upper Missouri*—The 6th regiment of infantry left Bell Fountain on the 4th October. Colonel Atkins commands the expedition. Thus the public have at length the satisfaction to see fairly embarked, this interesting expedition, on the security of which depends the accomplishment of such mighty objects of the American people, viz:—the transfer of the fur trade from the English to the Americans; the extinction of British influence among American Indians, and the opening a direct intercourse with India by the Columbia and Missouri rivers."

For several years past it has been a favorite object of the American government to open an easy communication from their western settlements to the Pacific Ocean, and the above paragraph indicates the steps which have been taken to realize this vast project. The most western settlements which the Americans have are on the Missouri, and from the mouth of the Columbia on the Pacific Ocean they are distant about 3,000 miles. This immense space of desert territory, inhabited by Indian tribes, some of whom are hostile, presents obstacles of no ordinary kind to this scheme; while, at the same time, it is this very circumstance of the country being a wilderness, over which the Indian, and the wild beasts of the forest range undisturbed, that offers such peculiar inducement to the American design, not of colonizing the country, though this consequence would undoubtedly follow; but of making

an immediate inroad on barbarism, by establishing a chain of posts at the distance of 50 or
100 miles along the great rivers as far as the Pacific Ocean. The fur trade is the great object of
attraction to settlers in this wilderness; and so
lucrative is this traffic, that it is well calculated to
excite a competition amongst rival states. It can
only be prosecuted by such nations as have a
ready access to these deserts, where the wild
animals which afford this valuable article of trade
multiply undisturbed by civilized man. These
nations are at present the British, whose possessions of Canada secures them access to the
north-western desert of America, the Americans,
who have free access to the wilderness that
lies between their territories and the Pacific
Ocean, and the Russians, whose immense empire
borders on the north-west coast of America, giving
them ample opportunities, which they have duly
improved, of establishing settlements on its shores;
of cultivating a friendly intercourse with the
natives, and of exchanging European articles for
the valuable furs which they collect in the course
of their hunting excursions. The fur trade has
been prosecuted with amazing enterprise and
activity by the British Canadian companies.
Every season they dispatch into the wilds a numerous body of their servants, clerks, and boatmen, amounting to about 800, who, traveling in
canoes across the vast succession of lakes and
rivers, which extend northwest nearly 3,000
miles into the American continent, and are connected with the great Canadian lakes of Huron,

Superior, and Ontario, etc., bring back a valuable supply of furs from these remote regions, in exchange for such European articles as are in request among their savage customers. This trade having been prosecuted with such success by the British, the Americans seem in like manner resolved to profit by the vast tract of similar territory to which they have access. By the journey of Captains Lewis and Clark across the Rocky mountains to the Pacific Ocean, the whole of that western region is now laid open. Numerous adventurers have since crossed, by easier and better roads, this mountainous barrier where they found an open champaign country, well wooded and watered, and abounding in game. Captains Lewis and Clark were often astonished at the immense numbers of wild animals which they met with in all directions, consisting of bears, wolves, beavers, hares, foxes, racoons, etc., and various other animals, which are keenly pursued on account of their furs.

The plan of the Americans seems therefore to be, to form settlements in this country with a view to a trade in its great staple, namely fur; and by establishing a port which would gradually grow up into a village or a town at the mouth of the Columbia River on the Pacific Ocean, they could thence transport their cargoes to the great Indian markets, in exchange for the valuable produce of the East. Such is the project contemplated, and if it succeed, it would have this important consequence, that it would lay the foundation of an American colony on the shores of the Pacific

Ocean. The peopling of the American continent is at present going on at a rapid rate; but by this means the seeds of population would be scattered with a more prodigal hand, and having once taken root, the shores of the Pacific would be quickly overspread with civilized inhabitants, drawing their support from the country in which they were settled, and in this respect independent of the parent state.

CHAPTER I.

*Arrival of the Ship Tonquin, of Boston, at the Colum-
bia River, with Settlers.—Loss of a boat, an officer,
and six Men, in sounding a Passage.—Loss of
another Boat and two Men.—Miraculous Escape of
a Blacksmith, and a Sandwich Islander.—Settlers
landed.—The Tonquin trades along the Northwest
Coast.—Dreadful Catastrophe.—Resolute conduct
of the Blacksmith.—His Fate, and Fate of the
Vessel and Crew.*

THE ship *Tonquin,** belonging to John Jacob
Astor, left Boston about the year 1811, with
settlers, for the purpose of forming an establishment on the Columbia River. On their passage out, they touched at the Sandwich Islands
to fill up their water casks, and procure a supply
of provisions. Captain Thorne encountered considerable difficulties from the disposition which
his ship's company evinced to leave the vessel at
these islands, and was even obliged to get the
settlers to keep watch over them to prevent desertion: the boatswain, Peter Anderson, by some
means, however, eluded the guard and escaped
to the shore. The *Tonquin* arrived off the mouth

* This pioneer ship of Astor's enterprise sailed from New York,
September 8, 1810, under convoy for a time of the U. S. frigate
Constitution. [ED.]

of the Columbia in March, 1811. Captain Thorne not being acquainted with the harbor, dispatched a whale-boat, with an officer and six men, to sound the passage over the bar into the river. The ship was then under close reefed top-sails, and a strong gale blowing from the north-west, so that the first officer was much averse to going on this service; and it is rather singular, that previous to his leaving the *Tonquin*, he observed to Mr. McDougal, who was to be the governor of the establishment, that he was going to lay his bones beside those of his uncle, who had perished in crossing the bar of the Columbia river a year or two before that time. In a quarter of an hour after they left the ship, they hoisted a signal of distress, and then disappeared—thus seven men found a watery grave! The *Tonquin* stood out to sea for the night, and in the morning again stood in, and another boat was ordered off under the command of the second officer Mr. Moffat, who peremptorily refused to go, observing, that he could see a passage better from the mast head. Captain Thorne then ordered a man, who was to have the command of a shallop (of which they had the frame on board), to take the command of the boat, with two Sandwich Islanders (several of whom they had on board for the establishment), the ship's blacksmith, and one sailor, Mr. McDougal having refused to let any of the settlers go on that service which they looked on as little better than an act of insanity. Shortly after the boat had left the ship, she ran by it; the boat was then so close that the people asked for a rope;

but the vessel herself was in so perilous a situation, that all on board had to attend to their own safety. She struck several times on the bar, and the sea made a fair breach over her; but they at length got under the north point, into Baker's bay. On the following day they saw a white man on the rocks, in the bay. Captain Thorne dispatched a boat, which returned with the blacksmith, who had been in the second boat sent to sound the channel. The account he gave of himself was, that shortly after the ship had passed them, the boat swamped; that the master of the shallop and the sailor were drowned, and that he was saved by the exertions of the Sandwich Islanders, who had dived several times to clear him of the lead line which was entangled round his legs. As the tide was ebbing strong, the boat drifted clear of the breakers; the islanders got a bucket and one of the oars; the blacksmith and one of the islanders took it in turns to scull the boat during the night. The other islander died in consequence of being benumbered with the cold, so that he could not exert himself as the others did. At day-light, they found themselves drifted to the northward of the river into a small sandy bay; they ran the boat on the beach and hauled her as high as their strength would allow them, and got their dead companion out. They then crossed the point towards the river, and entered the woods, where the islander lay down by the stump of a tree. The blacksmith left him, crossed the point, and arrived in sight of the river, where, to his inexpressible joy, he saw the ship at anchor in the bay.

Captain Thorne sent a party in search of the islander, whom they found. They also recovered the boat, and buried the other native. They then landed the settlers about seven miles from the entrance of the river, and on the south side, where they immediately commenced clearing away the woods, building a fort, block-houses, etc. to protect themselves against the Indians. The *Tonquin* next landed part of her cargo, of which Mr. McDougal took charge; and Mr. McKie* accompanied Captain Thorne to trade with the Indians to the northward. For this purpose, they sailed from the river and swept along the coast till they came to Woody Point, where they ran into a snug harbor, in latitude of 50 deg. 6 min. N. and longitude 127 deg. 43 min. W.; in this place they carried on a brisk trade with the natives, of whom Captain Thorne, however, allowed too many to come on board. Mr. McKie remonstrated, and pointed out the danger to which they subjected themselves, by placing too much confidence in savages. But the captain was above taking his advice, and permitted still more liberty in visiting the ship. On the morning of the fatal catastrophe taking place, he was awakened by his brother (whom he had appointed chief mate in the room of the one who was lost, while Mr. Moffat was left at the Columbia river to command the schooner or shallop), coming to inform him, that the natives were crowding on board in very great numbers, and without women, which was a sure sign of their hostile

---

* Irving's Astoria gives this name as McKay. [ED.]

96

intentions. Upon reaching the deck Captain Thorne was alarmed, and ordered the ship to be got under-way; four persons went aloft to loose the sails, while the remainder were heaving at the windlass. The Indians had seated themselves round the decks between the guns, apparently without arms; but while the sailors were in the act of heaving at the windlass, they gave a sudden yell, and drew long knives from their hair, in which they had them concealed, rushed on the men, and butchered every person on deck. Captain Thorne defended himself for some time, but was at length overpowered, after having killed several of his assailants. The people aloft, terrified by this slaughter, slid down by the stays, and got into the forecastle, where, by means of the loop-holes, they soon cleared the decks of the savages. They were for some time at a loss how to act, and it was at length resolved that three should take the long-boat, and endeavor to reach the Columbia river. The blacksmith being wounded, preferred staying on board, and endeavoring to revenge the death of his ship-mates: the three men accordingly took provision and arms, and left the ship, and pulled directly out to sea. The blacksmith then waved to the natives to return on board, having previously laid a train of gunpowder to the magazine, and got his musket ready to fire it. The Indians seeing but one man in the vessel, came off in great numbers, and boarded without fear. He pointed out to them where to find the different articles of trade; and while they were all busily employed breaking open boxes, loosing bales, etc., he fired the train, and jumped overboard. By this explosion was destroyed nearly the whole village. He was picked up by some of the canoes, and it is said by the natives, is still among them, but is never allowed to come near the sea-shore. It may appear strange that he was not put to some violent death; but the savages estimate too highly the value of a blacksmith, who repairs their muskets, makes knives, etc.; in short, he is the greatest acquisition they can have. With respect to the three men who escaped the massacre on board, not being able to weather Woody Point, they were driven on shore, and killed by the natives. The boat remains, together with the wreck of the *Tonquin*, to this day.

The former part of this account of the loss of the *Tonquin* I had from Mr. McDougal, the governor of the fort at Columbia river, and the remainder from the natives, with whom I have had frequent intercourse, and whom I invariably found it to my interest to use well, as they are sensible of the slightest attention, and are prone to revenge the slightest insult.

CHAPTER II.

Continuation of the Account of the First Settlements on the River Columbia.—A Party sent over-land from Boston to form an Establishment.—Arrival of the Beaver: Plan of the Natives to take the Vessel frustated by an Indian Woman.—Trading Voyage of the Beaver to Norfolk Sound: collects a valuable Cargo of Furs: arrival at China.—Loss of the Lark of Boston off the Sandwich Islands.—The North-west Company obtain possession of the Settlement. —Voyage, &c. of the Isaac Todd from London.— Melancholy Death of Mr, McTavish and four others. —Voyage of the Columbia, in which the author was chief Officer.—Alarming Mutiny: Arrival at the Columbia.

THE next attempt to form a settlement on the Columbia was made by John Jacob Astor, who sent a party over-land from Boston,* under the command of Mr. Hunt. They endured many hardships in crossing the stony mountains, and lost several of their number; but at length reached their destination, the Columbia, after the destruction of the *Tonquin.* The next vessel Mr. Astor sent out was the *Beaver*, a ship command-

---

* The narrator is in error in naming Boston as the place of departure both of sea and land expeditions. New York was the headquarters, and the *Beaver* left that port Oct. 10, 1811. [ED.]

99

ed by Captain Sole.* She arrived safe in the river, and found the establishment in great distress for provisions. On the ensuing night, not being properly secured, she went adrift, and was nearly wrecked on the bar; they, however, got her into the harbour next day, and commenced landing their stores.

After they had unloaded, and received on board such furs as had been collected, they only waited for a fair opportunity to cross the bar, to observe which, Captain Sole went on shore daily, on Cape Disappointment. The natives, meanwhile, formed a design for seizing him and his boat's crew while on shore, and at the same time send off canoes to take the ship. The plot was, however, most fortunately frustrated by an Indian woman, who was on board with one of the sailors, and communicated the whole design to her temporary husband. This affair put Captain Sole more on his guard: the woman was handsomely rewarded, and is still at Fort George. The *Beaver* left the Columbia river, and ran along the coast to the northward. She went into Norfolk Sound, where the Russians have an extensive establishment, and there traded with the colonists for seal-skins. They were also induced to visit the islands of St. Paul and St. George, which are situated inside a group of islands, called the Aluthean (Aleutian) or Fox Islands. Here the *Beaver* was nearly lost among the ice; but ultimately, after encountering many difficulties, she

* Also given as Sowle and Soule by other writers; the latter most likely correct. [Ed.]

arrived safe at Canton, with a valuable cargo of furs, and was laid up, on account of the war between the United States and Great Britain.

Mr. Astor next sent out the ship *Lark*, Captain Northrope, with instructions to touch at the Sandwich Islands; but when they got into their latitude, and were running down before the wind, it came on to blow very hard, which reduced them to a close-reefed main top-sail and fore-sail. The sea was running mountain high, and the ship being very crank, in the middle watch (which was kept by Mr. Machal, a relative of Mr. Astor's) she suddenly broached-to, and a sea struck her, which laid her on her beam-ends. The people lost no time in cutting away the masts, by which means she righted. Fortunately for them, the cargo consisted chiefly of rum for the Russians, and light goods, which, added to the number of empty water-casks on board, made the ship float light. After the gale had abated, they got the spare spars, and rigged one for a jury-mast. They also built a sort of stage on the forecastle, and, by means of a Sandwich Islander named Power, whom they brought from America with them, got a top-gallant-sail up from below, and set it on the jury foremast. They then cut the anchors from the bows, but afterwards felt the loss of them, managing nevertheless to steer the ship towards the Sandwich Islands. They remained nineteen days on the wreck, subsisting entirely on what the islander could get from the cabin, as he could not go down the main hatchway, on account of the casks drifting about; they also killed several sharks which were swimming across the vessel. At length, on the nineteenth day of their being in that distressing situation, they, to their great joy, discovered land, and were drifted close to Mowee, (Maui) in a smooth sandy bay. They now experienced the want of their anchors, which might have saved the ship. Some canoes came off, and some of the people landed, when the wind suddenly shifting, blew strong from the land, and the ship was drifted from Mowee (Maui) to the point of Morotoi* (Molokai), where she went on the rocks, and was soon knocked to pieces. The captain and remainder of the crew were rescued through the exertions of the islanders, and kindly treated by them. The natives saved, too, a great deal of the cargo, and the chief of Mowee (Maui), Namea Teymotoo, (Keeaumoku) having arrived, took charge of the whole. The news soon reached Owhyhee (Hawaii), and Tameameah, (Kamehameha) the king, dispatched orders to Teymotoo, (Keeaumoku) to send what goods he had obtained, and also all the white men to him. The white men were sent, but Teymotoo (Keeaumoku) never quitted the island while the rum lasted, for which he nearly lost his head, which he certainly would have done, had not his sister, named Ta'amano (Kaahumanu), and who was Tameameah's (Kamehameha's) head wife, exerted all her interest successfully in his cause.

The establishment on the Columbia River being so valuable in respect to the fur trade, it was

* This should be Kahoolawe, not Molokai. [ED.]

determined by the Northwest Company of Canada to get possession of it. It was therefore arranged to fit out a ship for that purpose, and accordingly the ship *Isaac Todd* was selected and equipped by Messrs. McTavish, Fraser and Company, merchants, commanded by Captain Smith. She left England in March, 1813, with a number of settlers on board, the principal of whom was Donald McTavish, Esq. There was also a party sent over-land from Canada to reach the Columbia about the same time at which it was calculated the ship would arrive. The *Isaac Todd* called at Rio de Janeiro, and sailed thence under the convoy of his majesty's ships *Phœbe*, *Racoon*, and *Cherub*, of which she lost sight off Cape Horn; and, after beating off the Cape for some time, and nearly getting ashore, the captain, settlers, and sailors continually fighting and quarreling, at length arrived on the coast of California. Most of the people being laid up with the scurvy, they determined to run into Monterey (the Spanish seat of government on California) to recruit their crew, of which there was scarcely a sufficient number well enough to work the vessel. They anchored in Monterey in the latitude of $36° 36'$ N., and longitude $121° 34'$ W.; got permission to land the sick, and were well treated by the Spaniards, and recovered fast. When they were about to leave Monterey, an officer came over-land from Port St. Francisco* to order the *Isaac Todd* round to that port, and enable the *Racoon* to heave down and repair.

---

* San Francisco.

She had arrived in the Columbia river, and found the establishment in possession of the party that came over-land, and the English colors flying on the fort. On the approach of the party, they had informed the Americans that some of his majesty's ships were coming to take possession of the place. Upon this the colony made the best bargain they could, and the English took possession of the fort, with a valuable assortment of furs. A few of the American clerks went on board the American brig *Pedlar*, but the governor, Mr. McDougal and the rest, entered into the service of the English Northwest Company. The *Racoon*, after having completed her wooding and watering, lay sometime in the river; on her crossing the bar, she struck, and so much damaged her bottom, that she could scarcely be kept above water till her arrival at Port St. Francisco, a distance not exceeding 500 miles from the Columbia. By means of the *Isaac Todd*, his majesty's ship was soon repaired, and sailed towards the Sandwich Islands. Several of the crew of the *Isaac Todd* deserted at Monterey, being afraid they should be pressed into the *Racoon*. She then sailed from Port St. Francisco, and arrived off the Columbia river in April, 1814, got over the bar in safety, and anchored in Baker's Bay. The *Todd* went up the river, and moored opposite the fort above Village Point; and all the entreaties of Mr. McTavish could not prevail on Captain Smith to bring the ship across: his excuse was, want of water in the channel, where there is three fathoms and a half at high tide.

The consequences were fatal; for, on Sunday, the 22nd of May, as Mr. McTavish was crossing the river in the vessels long-boat, under the charge of Captain Smith's nephew, when they got about mid-channel, they were upset by a sudden squall, filled, and sunk immediately. Mr. McTavish, Mr. Henry and four others, found a watery grave, and an American carpenter, named Joseph Little, alone saved himself with an oar. He drifted up the river, and got on the stump of a tree, whence he was taken by an Indian canoe to the fort, where he communicated the sad fate of the governor and party. Within a few days two of the bodies were picked up, and buried close to the fort, and shortly after, the body of Mr. McTavish was drifted ashore to the northward of Cape Disappointment, and a party was sent to bury him there, as it was not safe, at that time, to bring him to the fort, where the natives were very troublesome, and all collected from the northward to fish in the river, this being the season.

Having served my time in the West India trade with Captain Stoddard, in the employ of Messrs. Inglis, Ellice and Company, of Mark-lane, I arrived in London about August, 1813, from a West Indian voyage. The houses of Inglis, Ellice and Co. and McTavish, Fraser and Co., were then fitting out a vessel for the northwest coast of America and China. A schooner that had formerly belonged to the Americans, was purchased for this voyage, and called the *Columbia*. She was a sharp-built vessel, of 185 tons register, and had a crew of 25 men, officers included.

She was armed with ten nine-pounders, and had a patent boarding defence all round her bulwark. Her commander was Captain Anthony Robson, under whom I served as chief officer.

I went on board in August, 1813, and after taking our cargo on board, we dropped down to Gravesend the latter end of September, completed our stores, wood and water, at the Motherbank, and on the 26th of November, 1813, sailed under convoy of his majesty's ship *Laurel*, Captain Proby, in company with the Brazil fleet. On the 24th of January we crossed the equinoctial line in the longitute of 24 ° o' west, having much thunder, lightning, and rain. A strong current setting to the northward, on the 31st, we made the land about Pernambuco on the Brazil coast, spoke several catamarans, which are made of four or five logs of wood, trunneled together, and well lashed. They are rigged with a large lug-sail, and are used to fish and trade along the Brazil Coast, manned with four or five negroes. February 9th, we saw Cape Frio in the latitude of 23° 1' south, and longitude 41 ° 45' west, and on the 10th we came-to in Rio de Janeiro harbor. We lost no time in preparing to wood and water the ship, the season for doubling Cape Horn being far advanced; several of our crew deserted, and we had great difficulty in procuring others.

On the 19th of February, having completed our stores, etc., we sailed from Rio, intending to touch at the Falkland islands, and refit, previous to doubling the Cape. On the 14th of March we saw the Falkland Islands, stood away to the eastward, towards Berkeley's Sound, and as we sailed along shore, observed a great number of cattle and horses. About 11 o'clock P. M., we rounded Cape St. Vincent, and worked up the sound with a strong gale at S. W. At 3 P. M., came-to between Penguin and Goat Islands, at the head of the sound in six fathoms, soft bottom. I went on shore with a party on Goat Island, where we shot a number of ducks and other birds, of which there appeared to be great numbers, as also of the fur seal. Next day, Captain Robson went on shore to a town which we saw from the ship, apparently deserted. In the evening he returned with the boat nearly full of ducks and geese. We got under weigh, and warped nearer the place in four fathoms water, good bottom. It appeared that the town had been deserted by the Spaniards in 1811: they called the island *Soledada*. We found it well stocked with cattle, horses, ducks, geese, etc., and also a small quantity of cabbages and celery, the gardens being nearly chocked up with weeds, which we cleared away, and planted seeds of different kinds. On the 27th day of March, 1814, having completed the rigging, we took a stock of fresh beef, geese, and pigs on board, filled up our water, got under way, and stood out of the sound, with a strong S. W. wind. While we lay at these islands, the people had fresh beef, geese, and vegetables daily; and when we sailed, all on board were in good health, except our surgeon, who had been ill since we left Rio de Janeiro.

Cape St. Vincent and Cape Pembroke form the entrance of this sound; the former is in the latitude of 51° 26' south, and longitude 57° 54' west; the latter, in latitude 51° 56' south, and longitude 57° 54' west; the sound is about three leagues deep and about three miles wide in the middle. Ships bound into this sound must give Cape St. Vincent a wide berth, on account of a reef that runs about a mile off the point; and it would be particularly advisable for such as are going round Cape Horn, to touch here in preference to calling at Rio de Janeiro.

We encountered very severe weather going round the cape; at times not more than six or eight men were able to stand the deck, from being continually wet and cold, and the schooner being so low that the sea was continually washing over her. On one occasion, April 14, 1814, she shipped a sea that washed the round-house clean from the deck, and filled the cabin: we had four feet of water in the hold, and in this gale carried away the fore-yard, and split all our sails, so that, at one time, we had not a single sail that was fit to set. About the 18th of April, we doubled Cape Horn, and ran along shore to the northward, with a fine S. W. breeze. May 26th, John Jameson, the surgeon, departed this life, after a long illness: he was a native of Scotland, aged about 26 years. His body was committed to the deep with the usual ceremonies.

On the 22nd of May, we crossed the equinoctial line in the longitude of 109° 14' west, with a strong breeze from E. S. E. and fine weather. Nothing of moment occurred until the 22nd of June, when a young man, of the name of Thomas Smoke, came aft, and divulged a most villainous design, planned by four of the men, viz: John Happy, boatswain, John Carpenter, John Peterson, and John Decrutz, seamen. Their horrid purpose was to rise in the middle watch, which it happened I was to keep, and throw me overboard; one of the parties was then to go to the cabin, and dispatch the captain, who was at that time unwell, and the others were to murder the officers in the half-deck. They had asked Smoke if he could navigate the ship to the Spanish main for them: he answered that he could, and was thus enabled to frustrate their treachery.

Having put us on our guard, he went forward, but not below, and we made preparations for the villains in as private a way as possible. 'I wished to secure them immediately, but Captain Robson declined doing so till the morning, it being then dark. We armed all the officers in the half-deck, and opened a door which led from the cabin to that berth; we then unhinged the doors, and put them below. The second mate took the first watch from 8 o'clock to midnight, and the rest of us kept in readiness to jump on deck at the least notice. Midnight came, and I succeeded to the watch. I went on deck armed with three pair of pistols. My first care was to look round, and see that every thing was right; I then called down the forecastle, to know if the watch were coming on deck: the answer was, "Aye, aye, sir." Shortly after, Happy came on deck, and relieved the helm, but none of the others made their appearance. It being a fine night, I was glad they kept below, as it was my determination to shoot the first man who should attempt to come abaft the gang-way. At daylight we called them one at a time, and secured them in irons. Towards noon, Carpenter requested to be taken out of irons, and to make a confession concerning the mutiny. His deposition was accordingly taken by Captain Robson, and signed by the officers, after which we were obliged to keep him apart from the other prisoners, as they swore they would murder him.

Latitude 39° 14' north; longitude 134° 39' west. On the 29th of June, we made Cape Orford, on the coast of New Albion, and on the 6th of July we saw Cape Disappointment, the north point of Columbia River: latitude 46° 19' north, and longitune 123° 0' west. We stood close in with the bar, fired a gun, tacked ship in 6½ fathoms dark sand, about half a mile from the breakers. Next day we stood in: the tide setting in strong, and drifting us fast towards the bar, I went to the mast-head to look for a channel, and perceived an Indian canoe paddling towards us. She soon after came alongside, and the natives began talking to us in a language we did not understand; we then lowered the boat down, and I took one of the Indians with me to sound before the ship, —the least water we had was 3½ fathoms on the bar. On rounding Cape Disappointment, an Indian village opened to our view, consisting of about 50 miserable looking huts. The Indians were all busily employed, launching their canoes, and pushing off towards the ship, which was a novel spectacle to us all, as we had never seen people of this description before. At three o'clock P.M. we anchored under Cape Disappointment in Baker's Bay, about a mile from the village, and were soon visited by about 30 canoes, with men, women, and children, most of whom had flat heads. We put sentries on immediately, and ran our boarding defence out, to the great astonishment of the natives.

CHAPTER III.

The Schooner is repaired, and Mutineers sent into the interior; sail from the Columbia river.—Arrive at New Archangel or Norfolk Sound, and purchase a cargo of furs; return to the Columbia river, complete the cargo of furs for China, and of goods for the Spanish Main. Sail for Monterey for the purpose of forming a factory, to supply the establishment on the Columbia river with provisions.—Spaniards refuse to allow this, but suffer a cooper to remain to cure provisions.—Sail for Bodago.—Russians refuse to allow the gentlemen to remain till our return from Canton.—Arrival at Owyhee (Hawaii).—Visited by the king.—Natives crowd on board.—A summary method to get rid of them.—Two gentlemen of the N. W. Company land at Owhyee to wait our return.—Sail for and arrival at Canton.

THE natives on the Columbia brought us plenty of fine salmon, sturgeon, and fruit, such as strawberries, blackberries, rasberries, etc., for which we gave them, in exchange, knives, buttons, etc. We shortly after observed a remarkably large canoe, coming off with two Indians very finely dressed: they proved to be the king's sons, Casakas and Selechel, who made us signs that there was a three-masted ship above the point. We gave these people bread and treacle, of which they appeared to be very fond. Shortly after we perceived a schooner-boat beating down the river; and about 7 o'clock she anchored in-shore of us. I went on board of her well armed, and found Mr. Black, chief mate of the *Isaac Todd*, with several of the clerks belonging to the Northwest Company, whom I brought to the Columbia. The schooner was manned with Sandwich Islanders. The next morning we weighed and ran up the river, passed two Indian villages belonging to the Chenook tribe, and came too above Village Point, along-side of the *Isaac Todd*, in seven fathoms water, good bottom. Captain Smith visited us, and a large bark canoe came across from Fort George, in which was the governor, John George McTavish, Esq., with whom Captain Robson went on shore. Next day Captain Robson returned with a party from the fort to take the mutineers on shore; they were well guarded. After the necessary precautions, we then crossed the river in 3½ fathoms water, and anchored under Fort George in 6 fathoms water, very excellent holding ground. We were visited daily by Comley, king of the Chenook tribe, with his wives and family; and also by the other tribes about the river, bringing sea-otter and beaver skins, (which we were not allowed to buy from them), with plenty of fine salmon and sturgeon. During this time, the *Isaac Todd* had been taking in furs for China; on the 22nd of July, she was ready for sea, and dropped down

113

below the Point.   Mr. Bethune, one of the Northwest Company, went on board as supercargo
for China.   Having finished the rigging of the
schooner, we commenced taking in bar-iron,
rum, powder, ball, etc. for the Russian settlements to the northward.   Mr. James McTavish
came on board as super cargo; Mr. McLennan
as clerk.   Finding there were several American
ships on the coast, we embarked two long six-
pounders, and a brass four-pounder, with small
arms, etc., also three Sandwich Islanders who
were left here by the *Tonquin*, three Canadians,
an old man, who had been a long time in the
Russian Northwest Company's service, and a
half breed boy.   Having completed our cargo, we
took our wood and water on board.

On the 4th of August, eight bark canoes,
belonging to the Northwest Company, sailed
with stores for the posts in the interior, with
seven men in each canoe, including three of
our mutineers; the other being a blacksmith was
kept at the river.   On the 16th, both ships weighed
with a strong breeze from N. W., and turned
over the bar, in a heavy sea in 3 fathoms water.
In crossing, the sea washed over us, and left the
decks covered with sand.   We left the *Isaac
Todd* at anchor, and made all sail to the westward; we had a steady breeze from N. W. and
W. N. W.   On the 26th of August we had a
strong gale, sprung our bowsprit and fore-top-
mast; and, on the 29th, we saw Queen Char-
lotte's Island.   September 2nd, we made the
land, called, by the Russians, New Arch-

angel, and by the English, Prince of Wales's Archipelago; in the evening we were close in with the bay of islands, to the northward of Norfolk Sound. On the 5th, we entered the Sound by 10 o'clock, the wind dying away we got the sweeps on; fired several guns; at 11 o'clock we were boarded by a skin-boat, called bodaree, and a smaller one, called bodarkee; the latter was dispatched on shore to let the governor know what ship it was; the former assisted to tow us towards the harbor. When we got to the head of the Sound, we ran inside a group of islands, and came too off the Russian fort, in 3½ fathoms water, good holding ground: found here a fine American ship, called the *Packet*, Captain Bacon, with a valuable cargo of furs on board, which they had collected on the N. W. coast. We saluted the fort with thirteen guns, which was returned with the same number. Captain Robson, and the supercargo waited on the Governor Baranoff; sent the carpenter to cut some good spars for bowsprit and topmast. September 13th, the supercargo, having agreed with the governor, we commenced landing our cargo; by the 21st, we completed our rigging, wooding, and watering, took on board a quantity of fur, seal skins, and made all clear for sea. While we lay here a large Russian brig arrived, with a valuable cargo of furs, from the Aluthean, or Fox Islands; she had been two years on her voyage, which might have been performed in six months; also arrived here the sloop *Constantine*, from Kodiac, with furs and stores. At this time there were two large ships hauled on shore, undergoing some repairs; two large sloops ready for sea, and two gun-boats; a ship of 400 tons, which they had built here, was trading on the coast for furs; and a large brig and schooner trading on California. The Americans were very friendly with us, often spending their evenings on board. During our stay, we were well supplied with salmon, hallibut, and wild fowl.

It is the custom of Governor Baranoff to make his visitors drunk, when they dine with him. On these occasions he will commence firing guns, which must be answered by the ships, and I have often been obliged to fire upwards of fifty guns in a day. The governor dined on board once with his suite, and seemed much pleased with our boarding defence. The Russians have a fine fort on a high rock, mounting about sixty guns, and well calculated to defend them from the Indians; a good ship would, however, soon destroy it. They have also blockhouses, and a town of about sixty houses, a church, ship-yard, etc., and about 100 Russians, chiefly convicts from Siberia. They employ a great number of Kodiac and Oonalaska Indians to hunt the sea-otter and man their ships; they also hire American ships to take Indians and canoes to California, where the sea-otters are very plentiful, for the capture of which they allow the ships a certain proportion. They have also several hostages from the tribe about the Sound, and will not allow a canoe to come near the fort, without bringing a handsome present; they have a look-out house on the top of the fort, where a man is continually kept with a spy-glass in his hand, and if a canoe should heave in sight, a gun-boat is immediately dispatched after her. The town is enclosed by a high paling, and look-out houses built at the distance of twenty yards from each other, where there are people on the watch, both day and night. Every Russian has cleared a piece of ground, where they sow potatoes, turnips, carrots, radishes, sallad, etc., by which means, with plenty of fish and whale blubber, they live very comfortably, marrying the Kodiac and Oonalaska women, who are very industrious and make good wives. The Russians are extremely fond of rum, and will part with any thing for it; tobacco is also in great request. This country abounds with wood, chiefly of the pine kind. The hills are continually covered with snow, and it rains a great deal; we had not six fine days while we lay here. The whole of the population of this establishment does not exceed 1,000 souls.

September 27th. We made sail out of the Sound, and stood off towards Columbia river, on our passage to which nothing worthy of remarks occurred. We found the *Isaac Todd* had left the river on the 26th of September, 1814. The Chenook tribe of Indians were rejoiced to see us, and treated us in a very friendly way; then king Comley came on board as usual. I was therefore dispatched in the schooner-boat to bring the body of Mr. McTavish to the fort; which was done accordingly, and the corpse interred with funeral ceremonies. Captain Robson read the burial service; the coffin was lowered into the grave, which being enclosed all round with paling, a kind of tomb-stone was erected. While we lay in the river, we had much rain and thunder, with heavy gales from S. W. to S. E.

In November we finished a cargo of furs for China, and an assortment of goods for the Spanish Main; and having completed our wood and water, and taken on board plenty of spare spars, we at length cleared the dangerous bar, and stood off to the southward towards Monterey. On the 23rd of November, made the coast of California; saw the harbor of Sir Francis Drake, and the port of St. Francisco; passed the Farlone rocks, about one mile from them; at daylight, saw the north point of Monterey Bay; in the evening, it falling calm, we came too in the bay in 50 fathoms sand; at daylight a breeze sprung up, weighed and turned into the anchorage, we came too in 11 fathoms sandy bottom, about a quarter of a mile from Captain Vancouver's Observatory, and about the same distance from the fort. I went on shore to report the ship, and was kindly received by the Spaniards, who had all their force (about 50 horsemen) drawn up on the beach to receive me. I asked the governor if he would answer a salute; he complied, and I went on board and saluted with 11 guns, which was returned. Captain Robson and the gentlemen then went on shore, and sent off some fresh beef and vegetables for the crew. Mr. McDougal informed the governor that he wished to remain at Monterey, to collect provisions for the Northwest Company's establishment on the Columbia river. The governor could not grant him permission without receiving an order from the viceroy of Mexico; accordingly a courier was dispatched to Mexico, with letters to state our wishes to him. In the meantime, we had fresh beef and vegetables sent off daily. The people had liberty to walk and ride about the town, the Spanish men and women often coming on board. On Friday, the 16th of December, we received a final answer from Mexico to the following purport, viz; that they could not allow any gentleman to remain in the country; we might land the goods we had brought to barter, and the governor was to see to the collecting of provisions for us against our return from Canton; but the cooper was allowed to remain (as a great favour) to superintend the curing of the beef. With these terms we were obliged to comply. We accordingly landed the goods, consisting of bale goods, iron, sugar, tobacco, rum, etc. On the 17th, eight of our men deserted, and though we tried all means we possibly could devise to bring them back, we failed in that object. On the 21st of December we sailed from Monterey towards Bodago, a Russian establishment on New Albion, in the latitude 38° 0′ and longitude 123°, which we reached in due time.

On the 24th we saw a large storehouse on shore; Mr. McDougal and myself went in quest of its owners; we found it locked, and then pulled up a lagoon, where we saw a number of Indians collected round a large fire. We landed, and found ourselves *above* an Indian village, for here they live under ground, and we could hear their voices beneath us. Several old women and children made their appearance; we gave them some beads and by signs inquired where the Russians were; they pointed to the men round the fire, to whom we accordingly went up, and found them killing rabbits. Their mode of hunting them is to fire the grass for a considerable distance, and kill the rabbits as they are endeavoring to escape from the flame. The natives, on this part of the coast, appear to be a very harmless race. We inquired for the Russians, and they pointed to the northward. We then left them, and, on passing the village, some of our party had the curiosity to venture into their subterraneous abodes, but were obliged to make a hasty retreat, pursued by swarms of fleas, and an intolerable stench from a mass of filth.

We re-embarked, and made all sail to the northward, and at 4 P. M. were visited by some Russians in bodarkees; they brought with them a present of fresh pork and vegetables, and one of them piloted us to the settlement, where we anchored with the stream in 30 fathoms water, bottom of soft mud, about one mile from the shore. Mr. McDougal then went on shore to ask permission to remain until the schooner arrived from Canton, which was refused by Governor Kutscoff, without first getting permission from Governor Baranoff. He returned on board, and at daylight we weighed, and made sail for the Sandwich Islands.

January 7th, in latitude 27 north, we fell in with the N. E. trade-wind; on the 16th January, 1815, made the island of Owhyee (Hawaii), ran close in shore; some natives visited us, and informed us that Tameamah (Kamehameha) was at the village of Tyroa (Kailua). We made all sail for that place, and the next day ran between Owhyee (Hawaii) and Mowee (Maui), and stood close in shore. The natives came off in great numbers, bringing with them hogs, vegetables, rope, and cloth of the country; we allowed a few to enter the vessel, and took a chief woman on board, who acted as pilot. About midnight we reached Tyroa (Kailua), where we anchored in 30 fathoms water, very foul bottom; saluted the king. Mr. McDougal went on shore, and returned with the king next morning: Tameamah (Kamehameha) was dressed in a coloured shirt, velveteen breeches, red waistcoat, large military shoes, and worsted stockings, a black silk handkerchief round his neck, no coat: he is a tall, stout, athletic man, nose rather flat, thick lips, the upper one turned up; an open countenance, with three of his lower front teeth gone. We weighed anchor, and towed close in shore in 14 fathoms sandy bottom; the canoes collected from all parts, and, in a short time, there were no fewer than eighty of them, with from three to ten men in each, and some hundreds of men, women, and children swimming about the ship, regardless of the sharks; the decks were soon covered with them. Captain Robson, being rather alarmed at having so many on board, told the king to send them on shore. He took a handspike in his hand, and said a few words, and in a moment the men flew out of the ship in all directions. The king ordered us to hoist a white flag, which here signifies taboo, or prohibition, and then ordered two of his hikanees (aikanes), or confidential men, to remain on board, to keep the natives from stealing. The king, queens, and principal chiefs remained with us all day, and had their dinner sent on board to them, not being allowed to eat ship provision. It is a strange custom that any thing out of which the king eat or drank he had sent on shore. In the afternoon Captain Robson landed in company with his majesty, who gave Mr. McDougal permission to stop in his dominions as long as he pleased, and assured him that he should want for nothing. We accordingly forwarded their baggage, and the two gentlemen and a boy landed.

The king sent off a supply of hogs and tarrow, some very good island rope; and the same night, January 18th, we weighed and made sail for Canton. We made the islands of Bottel, Tobago, and Xima; and on the 5th of March passed Formosa, about two leagues from the valrette rocks; had wind, with much thunder, lightning, and rain. Next day, it being foggy, we sounded occasionally in from 35 to 20 fathoms of water, bottom of dark sand; when it cleared up, we were surrounded by Chinese fishing-boats, the sea being completely covered with them. On the 8th of March we passed Pedra Blanco, about one mile off, made the great Lema, and passed Antin.

On the 9th we ran into the Macao roads, and came too in 3½ fathoms water, bottom of soft mud. Captain Robson went on shore in a Chinese boat; in the evening he returned, and the next day took the young woman on shore, the Chinese not allowing her to proceed to Canton in the schooner. On the 17th of March, we got a pilot on board, weighed, and stood up the river; we were three days in our passage up to Wampoa.

CHAPTER IV.

Captain Robson gives up the command of the schooner Columbia; Captain Jennings appointed to succeed him.—Some particulars respecting Captain Jennings.—Sail from Canton.—Lost a man overboard. —Arrive at the Columbia river.—Massacre of three persons belonging to the Fort.—Assassins discovered and shot.—Another Voyage to Monterey; plenty of Provisions collected by the Cooper. —Description of the Town and Company.

AT Canton, Captain Robson found Mr. Bethune, and sixteen Sandwich Islanders, who had been left by the *Isaac Todd*. On March 28th, 1815, being quite tired of the northwest coast of America, and determined to go to England, he gave charge of the schooner to Captain Jennings, agreeably to an order from Mr. Bethune. Captain Jennings had left England in the brig *Forester*, and made an attempt to go round Cape Horn, but he did not succeed. At last they bore up for the Cape of Good Hope, going through the Straits of Tymore, the chief mate, with four of the crew, took the gig and left the ship in the night. After a tedious and troublesome passage, the *Forester* arrived off the island

124

of Woahoo (Oahu,) one of the Sandwich Islands, the crew being at that time in a state of mutiny. They saw several ships in the harbour, among which was the American schooner privateer, *Tameameah* (Kamehameha), Captain Porter. A canoe came off, and Captain Jennings intercepted a letter his crew were sending on shore, to say, that if the vessels in the harbour would send their boats out they should find friends. Captain Jennings immediately made sail towards Owyhee (Hawaii). On arriving, he anchored at Tyroa (Kailua), the residence of the king, who came on board with all his family, and on learning from the Captain his situation, promised him every assistance. He accordingly got the *Forester* under way, and ran to Karakakooa (Kealakekua) bay, where Captain Cooke was killed: here the Indians watered the ship, bringing the water down from the mountains in calabashes.

A very serious accident took place on board the *Forester* while she lay here. A boy ran away, but was brought back again, having lost all his clothes. One afternoon, when the ship was on the point of sailing, and Captain Jennings had occasion to go on shore, the boy went up to him and told him he wanted his clothes, and would not go to sea without them. The Captain promised that he would try to get them; and if not, some slops should be provided: the boy, however, would not be satisfied, and was extremely impertinent, which at last enraged Captain Jennings so much, that he gave him a box on the ear. Upon this the mutineer took hold of the Captain, who was a small man, and threw him down. The clerk, Mr. Ebbets, immediately knocked the lad down, and the boatswain espousing his quarrel, ran aft and struck Mr. Ebbets so violently as to stretch him on the deck. Captain Jennings then got clear, and called for irons to put on the boatswain, who remained quiet for some time. The irons happened to be too small, and the culprit having called for man's irons, went forward where he procured a long knife, and swore he would stab the first man that attempted to put him in irons. The Captain now seized a musket lying by the poop, presented it, and told him, if he did not keep quiet he would shoot him. The man opened his jacket, and bareing his breast, told the Captain to shoot and be damned; on which the latter fired, and shot him in the shoulder, with a bullet cut in four pieces. He instantly dropped, crying out "he was murdered." The crew were for rigging a whip to hang the Captain forthwith to the yard-arm; but while they were still debating the matter, Captain Jennings sprung from the ship into a canoe, and was paddled by the natives to the shore, where the king, Tameamah (Kamehameha), protected him. The wounded man was also taken on shore, but, from the want of proper assistance, mortification ensued; and as he would not allow his arm to be amputated, in a few days he died. Several of the crew left the *Forester*, vowing to be revenged. In the meantime, Mr. Biggot, the supercargo, took the command, and got one Adams to navigate and some islanders to work the ship. He then sailed from

Karakakooa (Kealakekua) bay for the coast of California, leaving Captain Jennings and five of the crew on shore. Some time after his majesty's ship *Cherub*, Captain Tucker, touched at Owhyee (Hawaii), under American colours, and the *Forester's* people, having ventured on board, were detained, while their late captain kept out of the way. The *Isaac Todd* arrived shortly after, and his voyage to Canton in her led to the arrangement I have just mentioned. I sailed upwards of three years with him on board the *Columbia*, and found him to be every way a proper person to command a ship in those seas.

Previous to sailing from Wampoa on the 28th of April, we took all the Sandwich Islanders on board; several of whom died shortly after. On the 2nd of May, we weighed from Macao Roads, and made sail for the Columbia River. On the 11th of May, we made the South Bashees; in the afternoon, ran between Grafton and Monmouth Islands: and on the 15th, passed the island of Majecosima, and several smaller islands. At this time, Joseph Ashton, one of the seamen, showed symptoms of insanity, and on the 17th, though he then appeared quite sensible and worked at the sails, he suddenly gave three Indian yells, and leaped from the lee-bow into the sea, where he was drowned. On the 26th, at midnight, we saw Moor's Island; bearing N. by W. 5 miles, latitude 30° 39' north, longitude 213° 30' west, on our passage from Canton hither we had the winds variable and much bad weather; passed drift-wood and sea-weed daily: as we approached the N. W.

coast, saw many large trees with their branches complete. Between the latitudes of 30° and 46° north, and longitude of 180° and 123° west, we saw many shoals of sperm whale. On the 21st of June we buried two islanders, and on the 1st of July crossed the bar of the Columbia, and anchored. At this time the river was full of Indians, and we were visited by them, bringing plenty of good salmon and berries. After we left the river, in November 1814, the natives had been very troublesome. A blacksmith and two men were sent a short distance into the woods to burn charcoal, where they commenced building a hut; several Indians collected about them apparently in a friendly manner, but the moment an opportunity offered, they took the axes belonging to the party and made a furious attack, cutting and mangling them most barbarously. They then made off, taking the axes with them; and the bodies were found next morning by some of the people. A strict inquiry was set on foot for the authors of this outrage, king Comley offering his services to find them; and at length, by the help of many valuable presents and some threats, two of the men were discovered. One of them was recognized by the Americans; he had on a former occasion been kicked from the fort for theft, and belonged to a tribe in the interior, denominated Soosoonies; and it was to revenge his disgrace that he persuaded some of his nation to join him and murder the men. The prisoners were confined in the bastion, and next morning led out, blindfolded, to be shot. They were placed opposite a 6-pounder, while a party of rifle-men were in the bastion ready to fire through the loop-holes, which manœuvre was made use of in order to make the Indians believe that they were shot by the great gun. The dead bodies were taken down to the wharf in coffins, and exposed for some days, till their friends were allowed to carry them away.

The *Columbia* now took another trip to Monterey, where we recovered our people who deserted when we were last here, and also four of the men that had deserted from the *Isaac Todd*. The former returned to their duty; the latter we confined for a while in irons. We found the cooper had not been idle; he had cured plenty of beef, and collected flour, beans, corn, tallow, pease, etc., the farmers bringing these provisions in daily. On our arrival a guard was posted at the landing-place to prevent smuggling; all trade, except through the governor, being prohibited. The Spaniards were not allowed to come on board as formerly, neither were our people allowed so much liberty on shore. The town of Monterey is most pleasantly situated on a beautiful and extensive plain, and nearly half a mile from a sandy beach. It consists of about 50 houses of one story, built in a square, surrounded by a stone wall, about 18 feet high; on the south side of the square stands the church; on the west, the governor's house; and on the east side, the lieutenant-governor's house and king's stores; on the north side is the grand and principal entrance, gaol, and guard-house, and in the middle are two field-pieces, 6-pounders. There are many farm houses scattered over the plain, with large herds of cattle and sheep; on the north side of the bay, is the river Carmel, which is full of excellent salmon and other fish. The fort stands on a hill, about one mile to the westward of the town; and just above the landing place, it is quite open on the land-side, and embrasures thrown up on the sea side mounting ten brass 12-pounders, with a good supply of copper-shot. At the landing-place, close to Captain Vancouver's Observatory, is a battery of two long 9-pounders, manned by about thirty soldiers. The governor, and a few others, are old Spaniards; the remaining inhabitants are Creoles of the country. They keep the Indians under great subjection, making them work very hard, chained two and two: the whole population of Monterey does not exceed 400 souls. About four miles to the southward, stands the Mission of Carmel; and about twelve miles to the northward, is the mission of Santa Cruz. The bay is sheltered from east to west, lying open to the northerly winds; the best anchorage is in seven fathoms, the fort bearing west, half a mile from the shore, The country is well wooded with pine and oak, but badly watered. There are many bears, wolves, foxes, deer, beavers, etc., and in the winter the ducks and geese are very plentiful, The bullocks are sold at four dollars each, and the sheep at one; two ships touch here annually for tallow, and to bring supplies for the establishments on California.

CHAPTER V.

HAVING returned to Columbia from Monterey, we speedily discharged our cargo,
and took on board a fresh one for Norfolk
Sound. The 16th of September, having completed our wood and water, we sailed for that
place. On the 18th, the people refused to do
their duty, alleging that they had not provisions
enough, though their allowance was five pounds
of bread, three pounds of pork, six pounds of
beef, and two and one-fourth pounds of flour per
week, with peas and beans; tea morning and

evening, and a quarter of a pint of rum per day. We called them aft to know their grievance, and after giving them a severe reprimand, ordered them to their duty, to which they went quietly. We were of opinion that the *Isaac Todd's* people headed this business, of which, however, we heard no more, as they found the officers were determined not to be trifled with. On anchoring in Norfolk Sound we found four American vessels lying there, from whom we learned that the war with America was at an end. The names of the Americans were the *Okean*,* the *Isabella*, and *Albatross*, formerly employed under the Russian flag, in the sea-otter fishery on California; the schooner *Liddy*, with a cargo from Canton for the Russians, and the brig *Pedlar*, commanded by Mr. Hunt, the individual who crossed the Stony Mountain. The *Pedlar* was seized by the Russians for selling powder to the natives in the Sound, but was given up before we sailed, (after several attempts to get out,) on the 17th of October, 1815. The ship *Isabella* sailed at the same time, while Dr. Shefham (Scheffer), a Russian, and some settlers for the Sandwich Islands; it being their intention to obtain footing there, as they had done on the coast of New Albion, the N. W. coast of America, and the Aluthean Islands. The Sandwich Islands indeed, would answer the purpose of west India Islands for them, as they are so conveniently near the N. W. coast of America, of the whole of which I am of opinion the Russians will possess themselves in time.

---

* Given by other writers as O'Cain. [Ed.]

On the 25th of October, we again entered the River Columbia, and sent the furs on shore to be re-packed. In November, nine bark canoes arrived with furs from the interior; on the 10th we received our cargo on board with stores, etc., and on the 13th, made sail for the Sandwich Islands. Nothing remarkable occurred on our passage, and on the 10th of December we made the Island of Owyhee (Hawaii); the ship was surrounded with canoes filled with articles of trade. On the 12th we came too off the village of Tyroa (Kailua), half a mile from the Morai (temple) on the point. Found the American ship *Milwood* here, purchasing sandal wood at the rate of 7 dollars for 133 pounds. The King, Tameameah (Kamehameha), came on board with the gentlemen we left last year, who had been well treated by the natives and wanted for nothing. On their first landing, the King had houses built for them, and gave them servants to attend on them. His Majesty and the Queens were rejoiced to see their old friend, Captain Jennings, and after taking a good proportion of wine they went on shore together. The Prince Reoreo (Liholiho) and his step-sister Maroo (Kamamalu) also visited the vessel; the Prince was accompanied by one of the chief priests; he was highly tatooed, and would not go under deck for fear the sailors or natives would walk above him. Being the greatest man on the island, no person was allowed to put even a hand above his head on pain of death. His sister was not so ceremonious, but came below and took her wine with me, and pressed me very much to remain on Owyhee.

133

The Russian had arrived and were on shore. Dr. Shefham (Sheffer) assured the King that he merely came to collect plants and see what the Island produced. During our whole stay, our decks were continually crowded with natives. We shipped a large quantity of island rope, which makes excellent running rigging; and the people were employed killing and salting pork; the King Queens, Prince and Princess coming on board daily and remaining until evening. Wanting to overhaul the rigging and caulk the ship, we determined to run down to Woahoo (Oahu), where there is a fine close harbour. We acquainted the King with our intentions, and he sent one of his hikanees (aikanes) or confidential men on board, named Kenopoo, to accompany us and see that we should get what we wanted. On the 16th of December we took leave of Tameameah, (Kamehameha) and with the ship full of men, women, and children, made sail for Woahoo, passed the Islands of Tahoorooa (Kahoolawe), Raini (Lanai), and Morokoi (Molokai), and on the 18th arrived at Woahoo (Oahu). We were boarded outside by John Young, a white man, who had lived on these islands upwards of 33 years: he piloted us into the harbour and we moored close to the shore, where thousands of the natives were collected, and soon crowded us. Mr. Manning (Manini), a Spaniard, and Mr. Harbottle an Englishman, who had been on the island for many years, came on board, as did also a number of respectable white men. This being Sunday we gave the people liberty to go on shore; one of the men, who left the *Forester* at Owyhee (Hawaii), came back with them, and remained. Next morning at sunrise we fired two muskets and sent the women out of the ship, and at sundown did the same as a signal for them to come on board; this practice we continued, and by that means kept the ship clear of natives. By the 29th of December we had completed repairing the rigging, caulked and painted the ship inside and out, and salted a quantity of pork; we then left these friendly people, and made sail towards Mooi* another of the group. 1st of January, 1816, we were close in with the village of Whymea (Waimea); Mr. Bethune, Mr. McDougal, and Mr. McLennan went on shore; Peter Anderson, who had been boatswain of the *Tonquin* and left by her at Owyhee (Hawaii), came to us, and was shipped as boatswain. We stood off and on the village all night, and the next day ran in between the reefs; the natives came off in great numbers, bringing hogs, goats, and vegetables to barter. The King, Tamoree (Kaumualii), did not make his appearance, but sent his head man to measure the schooner. On the 4th our gentlemen came on board, and we sailed for China, where we arrived on the 11th of February. The grand mandarin came on board to measure the vessel, and made the usual present of two lean bullocks, ten jars of sour stuff misnamed wine, and ten bags of something they call flour; they were not worth the trouble of taking on board, and I sold them to the compradore for two dozen geese.

---

* Though misnamed, the Author here refers to the island of Kauai. [ED.]

April 30th.—Weighed and made sail from Macao towards the N. W. coast of America. On the 23rd of May we passed Ormsby's Peak, a very high rock that makes like a ship in full sail, and is quite covered with birds, latitude 30° 48' north, longitude 217° east. On the 31st, we lost a young man, named James Dodd, overboard from the main-boom; the ship was then running ten knots per hour, with a strong fair wind; we immediately rounded-too and lowered a boat, but the sea ran so very high that she could not approach the man, who sunk, and it was with great difficulty we recovered the boat by making several tacks to windward. Our passage was the quickest ever made. July 11th, we saw Hallibut Island; also a remarkable volcano on the main land, from which a column of smoke ascended. Stood along towards the Straits of Oonalaska, and next day were close up with the island of that name. Tacked one mile from the west side of the Straits, wind blowing in hard squalls from N. W.; all the islands in sight were covered with snow; three bodarkees, with Oonalaska Indians, came on board, abreast of Cook's harbour. They had been out fishing, and returning home; they gave us some fish and we gave them rum in exchange. July 17th, off the island of St. George, we were boarded by two bodarkees, with one Russian and four Indians; next day we got off the landing place where there was a considerable store, a large bodarkee came on board and took the cargo onshore, and by the evening we had taken on board 313 bales of fur seal-skins. The Russians brought us off plenty of gull's eggs, salted ducks, and a number of young sea lions, which we found very good eating.

The islands of St. Paul and St. George are within sight of each other; the Russians keep 12 men on each, for the purpose of curing the fur-seal-skin, with which these islands abound. They take 40,000 annually, and still the seal does not decrease. The mode they pursue is as follows: The seal comes on shore to pup in July, and stays the whole summer, leaving a sufficient number of clapmatches and wigs; the hunters drive up the last year's pups like a flock of sheep, out of sight and hearing of the old ones, and knock them on the head; taking care not to let one of those driven up escape. Each summer's pups go to sea and comes on shore next summer, and are fit to kill. They leave the islands in November very lean; they take in several smooth stones about the size of an egg, I suppose for ballast. I could never find out where the seal winters; but certain it is, they must have a place where they remain during that season and feed, which has not yet been discovered. The people on these islands live under ground; they collect drift-wood enough in summer to last the winter; they live chiefly on sea-lion meat jerked, pickled ducks, gull's eggs preserved in oil, etc.

On the 24th we saw the ship-rock, and could hear the roaring of the sea-lion and elephant, long before we could see the rock, it being very foggy. On its clearing away, we saw the island of Oonalaska, and stood towards Cook's Straits.

The next day it came on to blow hard from S. E.; made sail for the harbour, black whale blowing in all directions; we found a snug town, church, etc., the natives were all employed drying salmon for the winter. Captain Jennings and the gentlemen accompanied the governor on shore; they took some rum with them to treat the Russians, who have a numerous herd of cattle and make excellent butter and cheese. They keep two skin-boats constantly employed in summer, collecting the drift-wood about the island, which is the only fuel they have. We lay here until the 29th, when we made sail towards Cook's Straits. While we lay about these islands we had not more than three clear days.

The Island of Oonalaska is in the latitude of 53° 55' north, and longitude 166° 22' west. The island is the chief depot for all the furs collected on the Aluthean Islands; and appears quite barren, without the least sign of wood. There is an excellent harbour, off the N. W. side, capable of holding several hundred vessels, and completely land-locked. The town consists of about twenty houses, a church, and some large sheds for the purpose of drying salmon and other fish. There are about twelve Russians here; the remainder of the inhabitants of the town are Kodiacs, and natives of the island, all converts to the Greek church. The natives of these, as well as of all the Aluthean Islands, are low in stature, broad, flat faces, with black eyes, and coarse black hair. Their dress consists of a loose frock, made of the skins of ducks and other birds, sewed neatly together; this part of the dress is the same in both sexes. When the men go in their canoes to hunt or fish, they wear a dress of the entrails of the seal; it is made like a large loose shirt, with a hood, and is water-proof. They also wear trowsers and boots, made from the throat of the sea-lion or elephant, which are water-proof also. They are extremely fond of ornaments, particularly of beads, with which they ornament their garments and person; they wear them round the neck, and pendant from the nose and ears, through which many holes are made. The men have a helmet or cap, ornamented with the beard of the sea-lion and with seed-beads. All the natives use paint. There are several villages about the harbour, but the island seems very thinly peopled, owing, I suppose, to the number that are employed by the Russians on their establishments on the N. W. coast of America Their canoes or bodarkees, are made from the skins of the hair-seal, stretched over a light wooden frame, leaving one, two, or three holes on the top for the sitters; the frame is sometimes of whalebone, and the vessels are from 10 to 16 feet long, and about 3 feet wide in the middle, gradually tapering towards the ends. They are pulled with great swiftness by a double paddle, about 12 feet long, with a blade at each end, and held by the middle; they are generally made of ask. The canoes perform voyages along the coast for several hundred miles, for the purpose of hunting the sea-otter and seal; they also kill black whales, which are about these islands in great plenty. If in their hunting excursions they are overtaken by a gale of wind, they lash all their canoes together in form of a raft, and in this manner float lightly on the top of the sea without the least danger. The large boats, or bodarkees, are made from the skins of the sea-lion or elephant, stretched over a stout wooden frame, open at the top, and are capable of carrying 50 or 60 men. In these boats they go to all the Aluthean Islands, to collect the furs; and sometimes to the main land, for timber. In catching the sea-otter and seal, these people are very dexterous; they conceal themselves behind the rocks, and throw out a seal-skin blown, with a line affixed, and draw it gently towards the shore: the seal or sea-otter following till within reach of their spears, they are easily captured. In hunting, they wear masks and skins to represent the beasts they are in pursuit of; they always carry a rifle with them, in the use of which they are very dexterous. All of them are extremely fond of rum, and they often part with their garments and hunting utensils, to purchase a small quantity. Their principal food consists of the black whale; also salmon, cod, hallibut, herrings, etc. When these fish are in season, they cure sufficient to last them through the winter, by drying and smoking them, without salt; they also eat their victuals without it; and the reason they give is, that it hurts the sight. Whether this be the case or not, all the natives are very sharp-sighted. On this island they have about 40 head of fine cattle, first imported from the Spanish Main; they have also some large hogs, which are fed on fish, and consequently not very delicate.

CHAPTER VI.

The Winter of 1816, on the Columbia River.—Alarming Fire.—Sail for the Sandwich Islands.—Account of the Columbia.—Manners and Customs of the Natives.

IN August, 1816, we once more touched at the Columbia, unloaded, and refitted.   We lived in tents on shore, within a fence erected to keep the Indians from stealing our tools.   On the 3rd of September our cook died, after four months' illness.   On the 9th, two canoes, belonging to the Northwest Company, arrived from the interior; they had left the brigade, consisting of nine canoes and about seventy men, encamped at Oak Point, sixty miles up the river.   On the 1st of October, the whole brigade of canoes arrived with furs; and, on the 5th, they again sailed (well armed) with stores for the interior, under the direction of Mr. McKenzie.   At this time, the season is wet; we therefore built sheds for the carpenters to work under; and, to the middle of November, all hands were working hard to get the vessel ready for sea before the winter set in.

November the 21st, we were much alarmed by a fire breaking out, about seven o'clock in the evening, at the fort; we lost no time in hastening to their assistance with our buckets, and in the course of half an hour got it completely under with the loss of only one house. Providentially, it was raining very hard, as, if there had been the least wind, the whole place must inevitably have been destroyed, with all our rigging, sails, stores, etc., and we should have been left at the mercy of barbarous Indians, without the means of helping ourselves. On the breaking out of the fire, the natives all fled from the village, making a dreadful noise.

December 1st, our hull being complete, we hauled off in the stream to take our masts in after having lain on shore for nearly four months. The first month of our stay here, the weather was delightful, and we were well supplied with excellent salmon and sturgeon, and a variety of small fish. Latterly we had much rain, thunder and lightning, heavy gales of wind from S.W. to S.E. The N.W. winds prevailed here in summer, and, in the winter, from S. W. to S. E., with thick, rainy weather. While here, I employed an Indian hunter. who, with my finding powder and shot, supplied the ship with ducks, geese, and swans, for one blanket. He furnished me so largely, that I made him a present of the musket, when I left the river, for which he was most grateful, and made me many presents.

On the 6th, of January, 1817, Lewis Lapham, our armourer, died, truly regretted, as he was a very serviceable man. On the 10th, we crossed the bar and got safe to sea. And now, while the ship is making for the Sandwich Islands, I shall endeavour to give an account of the Columbia River, with the manners of the people.

Cape Disappointment forms the north point of the river; it is in the latitude of 46° 19' north and longitude 123° 54' west; it is high, bluff land, very remarkable, and covered with wood. On that part which faces the S.W., there are a great many dead trees; and the bluff, or face of the cape, is quite bare. Point Adams forms the south side of the river; it is a low point, about seven miles from Cape Disappointment, in a S.E. direction, with a number of trees scattered over it. There is a sand-bank which runs from Point Adams to within two miles of the cape, and also another which runs from point Disappointment, in a S.W. direction, about two miles; this bank, of course, lies considerably outside the other, and the two are formed by the sea heaving up the sand when the wind sets in strong from the S.W., when, for some days, the sea breaks from point to point without any channel, and after the wind abates, the channel is again opened by the tide, which strikes Cape Disappointment, turns off in a S.W. direction, and divides both sands. Ships going into the river, may stand in without fear in mid-channel, till they bring the easternmost bluff of the cape to bear N. E., then haul up for it immediately, and, if bound into Baker's Bay, keep close.round the cape, and come too in five fathoms, the cape bearing south. Upon getting into the bay, you lose the tide; if bound up the river, run out of the bay, and bring Tongue Point open about a ship's length, with Chinook or

143

Village Point, the former makes like an island, and is about seven miles above point Adams, on the south side of the river; the latter is a remarkable hill, about seven miles above Cape Disappointment, known by a large clear patch on the side, and the only clear piece of ground in sight. In mid-channel, you have from seven to nine fathoms sandy bottom. In beating up or down, come no nearer the shore than four fathoms, or farther off than thirteen fathoms, which you will have on the edge of the banks; there is good anchorage above Chinook Point, in eight fathoms. The river is full of sand banks, formed by the numerous small rivers that branch off in various directions from the main one. The country, on both sides, is formed of impenetrable woods, chiefly pine, elder, maple, and birch trees; further up, there are plenty of good oaks and ash. The first tribe of Indians we saw were called the Chickeloes, under a chief, named Calpo. They come from a place called Classet, to the northward of the river, on the sea coast, and bring otter and beaver skins to trade at the fort. They encamp in Baker's Bay, and continue, from June to October, curing salmon and sturgeon for the winter. They are a very warlike people, and extremely dangerous, taking every advantage if you are off your guard. So hostile and treacherous were they, that we never allowed the men of this tribe to come on board.

About five miles up the river, on the north side, stands the Chinook village. The king of this tribe is called Com Comly, or Madsaw, which, in the Chinook tongue, signifies Thunder. The village consists of about thirty houses, built of wood, and very large; they are formed of boards, with the edges resting on each other, and fastened with stripes of bark to upright posts, which are stuck in the ground on either side of them. Some have ridge-pole and rafters, but the chief part are nearly flat on the top; they have old mats spread inside and out, to keep out the wind and rain. In every house there are from five to fifteen families, and each family has a fire in the middle of the building. On the sides they have their bed places, raised about a foot from the earth, and covered with mats; where they *pig in* all together, men, women, and children. The houses are decorated with rude carved images, which they call *clamas*, or gods, but they do not seem to pay any kind of homage or attention to them. Their furniture consists of boxes or chests, hollowed from the solid wood, of all sizes, and curiously carved; and of a number of baskets, which they work so close as to hold water. In the boxes they keep their property and spare garments, and also their dry provision. When the Indians shift to their winter quarters, they carry all the planks and mats of their houses with them, leaving nothing but the rafters and frame standing. They are filthy to the extreme; allow whole piles of fish entrails and other uncleanness to lie in the middle of the houses, never attempting to clear it away. Even in their eating they are very nasty; I have frequently seen them with a piece of meat, half roasted, in the dirt and ashes, lying on the ground with their feet on it, and tearing like wild beasts with their teeth. After their fish is boiled, they turn it out on a mat, or, if they have not got one readily, on the ground, and collect round it like a pack of hounds, devouring dirt and all. Their mode of boiling fish, vegetables, etc., is rather singular, and deserves to be related. They put whatever is to be cooked into a basket, and, nearly filling it with water, place it on the ground; they then proceed to boil or sodden it, by putting in red-hot stones (of which they have a number for the purpose) in quick succession, until the victuals are done to their satisfaction.

The chief employment of the men is to hunt and fish; they are, however, generally speaking, very lazy, and their young men lie basking in the sun, on the sides of the river, for hours together. The women and girls are employed in making hats, mats, etc., and in collecting berries and wood. These people have not the least notion of tilling the ground; they trust to Providence for every thing, and derive their chief support from the river and sea. They collect plenty of berries and fish in summer to last them through the winter. The former they preserve by mixing them up with salmon or seal oil, and, making them into lumps, set them to dry in the sun. When sufficiently dry, they are laid by in boxes and baskets for winter. The salmon they cure by splitting it up into four slices, and running splinters of wood across them. These they also dry in the sun, and then hang them up in the houses, where they are soon smoked and laid by for use. They are cured without salt, which is never used. The Indian women are complete drudges, yet they seem to work cheerfully. They have a root here like the potato, called by the natives wapitoe; it grows chiefly in swampy ground, and is collected in September.

The men are very stout and hardy; their height from five feet to five feet eight inches, well proportioned, and with very little beard. They wear a dress made of the skins of the wood-rat, sewed neatly together and thrown over the shoulders; this garment is the same in both sexes (with the addition of a petticoat, which the women wear.) It goes under the right arm and above the left, where it fastens with a wooden skewer, being open down the side, so that it leaves both arms at liberty for the use of their weapons. Their ears are perforated in many parts, and small bits of leather fastened in, from which hang shells in shape not much dissimilar to a game cock's spur, and about one inch in length. These shells are called hiaqua. The nose is also perforated, from which beads are suspended; and sometimes a large goose or swan's quill is pushed through. They anoint their bodies with a sort of red ochre and seal oil; and are very expert in the use of the bow, bludgeon, and dagger. Their bows are made of pine, about four feet long, and, in the middle, two inches broad, tapering off towards each end. The sinew of the elk is laid on the back of the bow, which bends it the contrary way and strengthens it; the string is also made of the sinew of the elk, and it requires a man of some strength to string them. The Chinooks are very expert in the use of this weapon; they will stand on the deck and stick an arrow into the truck with ease. Their arrows are made of light wood, and pointed with stone, bone, glass, ivory, or iron. Those barbed with ivory I have seen pierce a three-quarter of an inch plank at twelve yards distance. One day some of our people were practising the bow on board; they stood aft, and endeavored to strike a small looking-glass placed on the bow of the vessel, but none of them could succeed. An Indian, who was standing by, laughed most heartily at them, and taking up his bow, stood on the stern, and shooting, broke the glass in pieces, at a distance of 95 feet, the mark being about three inches square. The bludgeon is made of bone or iron, about two feet long, and stout in proportion, and handsomely carved and ornamented; the daggers are made of flint-stone or iron, and are held by the middle, so that they use both ends. The natives have a kind of loop to the bludgeon and dagger, which goes over the wrist, to prevent their being wrenched out of their hands; and they never stir out without one of these weapons. Their original tools are chisels made out of the pine knot, axes of stone, and stone mallets. With these they split large cedar trees into planks, with which they build their houses. Their canoes are very simple; some are large enough to carry 30 people, being about 40 feet long, the middle nearly six feet broad, and becoming gradually narrower toward the end.

They are about two feet deep, handsomely ornamented and painted; the ornamental parts are the
teeth of the wolf and sea-otter, which navigators
have taken for human teeth. The paddles are
made light and small, the length generally 6 feet,
of which 2½ feet forms the blade; the lower end
is forked like a fish's tail, and the upper end is
crutched very neatly. In the canoes they keep
nets, hooks, harpoons, and fish-gigs, etc., also
long spears for spearing salmon. The Chinook
women are short and very stout, with thick and
often bandy legs. Their hair, which is jet black,
they allow to hang loose all round their heads
and over their shoulders, never cutting it off
unless at the death of some near relative. They
wear, as I have noticed, a petticoat made of
rushes twisted over a string, with ends hanging
loosely down. This garment reaches the knee,
and keeps them very warm. The war-dress of
the men is made of the elk-skin, which is dressed
in the interior; it is very thick and yet pliable; an
arrow cannot penetrate it, and I have even tried
with a pistol-ball at the distance of 12 yards without effect, It is worn exactly as the common
dress, but is doubled about the body. The men
also wear a hat in the shape of a cone, with a
string that fastens under the chin. These people
have a horrid custom of flattening the heads of
infants. When a child is born, they lay it in a
small canoe or cradle made for that purpose;
they then fix a pad on the forehead and bind it
tight down, and keep it so till it broadens the face
and forces the eye out, giving them a most fero-

cious appearance. When the child screams with pain, they loosen the bandage and hold it to the breast; the flatter the head is, the greater the beauty in their estimation. Polygamy is allowed, and they keep three or four wives; they are not jealous, and so far from being at all delicate, they allow their women to go on board ship, and remain for weeks, taking care, however, to be well paid beforehand. Their mode of burying the dead is to fasten them in a small canoe with all their property, and hang the vessel up between two trees or stakes; they then cover them with mats.

CHAPTER VII.

Royal Family.—Anecdote.—Native Tribes.—Religious Ideas.—Habits.—Climate.—Traffic.—Slave Trade by the Americans; their Practices; instance of Captain Ayres.—Animals; War Canoes.—Voyage to the Sandwich Islands'; notice of several of these. —The King's Mercantile Speculations.—New Russian Establishment.—Method of curing Pork.— Norfolk Sound.—Jealousy of the Russians.— Native Women.—Hostility between the Natives and Russians.

COM COMLEY, king of the Chinook nation, is the richest and most powerful chief on the river; he is a short, elderly man, blind of one eye; he has three wives, and many children. His eldest son (Cassacas) is a strong, well-made man, about 5 feet 6 inches high; he succeeds his father in the government of the Chinooks; he is no friend to white men; he styles himself Prince of Wales. Selechel is the next son; he styles himself Duke of York; he is a small man, and well disposed towards the whites. While we lay in the river, a man belonging to a tribe in the interior, called Soosoonees, came to Chinook, and fired an arrow at Com Comley while bathing

151

in the river, and fled to the woods. The king instantly dispatched his head slave (who was a favourite) in pursuit of the man who had crossed over to the fort; the slave came up with him at the entrance of the woods, and with one blow of his bludgeon brought him to the ground, and dispatched him with a dagger. He then painted himself black, tied his hair up in a bunch, bound his arms and legs with grass, and went through the woods for three days and nights, crying the war-hoop, as a challenge of defiance. In the night we were much alarmed at the dreadful yelling, and put ourselves on guard against the worst, having seen many war canoes hovering about, and all the natives making warlike preparations. King Com Comley, however, made it up with the party, and prevented bloodshed.

A little above Com Comley's village is another belonging to the Chinook tribe, under a chief called Tackum, consisting of about 30 houses. On Point Adams there is a large village and tribe denominated Cladsaps, who differ in nothing from the Chinooks; these, with the Chickeloes, are the only tribes about the entrance of the river. All these people are superstitious to an excess, believing in spirits and supernatural agency. Apparently they have no professed religion, though they universally acknowledge one good spirit, who governs all things; and when it thunders they say he is angry. They also believe in an evil spirit, and in rewards and punishments hereafter. A confused idea prevails among them, that the world was destroyed by water, and will be again destroyed by the same element. They say, that when a good man dies, he goes to a world where there is plenty of provisions, and where there is no occasion to work; and on the contrary, when a bad man dies, he will go to a country where the provisions are scare, and where he will be forced to work hard, and meet with many and great difficulties. It may be gathered from this what is indeed the truth, that these Indians have a very great aversion to work. They observe the rite of circumcision, and have slaves whom they purchase from other tribes, prisoners who have been taken in war. On the death of a chief, from three to six slaves are sacrificed, according to the rank of the deceased. In the winter season all the tribes move back to the woods, where they have their winter villages. In summer they catch sturgeon, salmon, and a variety of small fish, etc.; in the fall of the year they have plenty of ducks, geese, and swans, and in spring an abundance of small fish like sardines. The climate is much the same as in England: from May till October the weather is very fine, the wind generally blowing from N. W. to N. E. The wet season commences in November with heavy gales from S. W. to S. E. with much rain and thunder. In some seasons the frost sets in early in November, and lasts for a month or two, after which the rains commence, and continues for the same time. During summer many of the tribes from the interior visit the fort with furs, and always encamp in a small bay close to it, where they are protected. Disputes frequently occur between these tribes and King Comley's tribe, in consequence of their having diverted some of the trade out of his hands. He used to take goods up the country, and trade with the tribes there, bringing the furs to the fort, where he had a profit of nearly half, so that it was to his advantage to keep them from the fort, by telling them the white men were bad, and would take them off and make slaves of them. I am sorry to say that the slave trade is carried on, on this coast, to a very great extent by the Americans. They buy slaves to the southward and take them to the northward, where they exchange them for the sea otter and other furs. If they cannot buy the slaves cheap, they make no scruple to carry them off by force. A Captain Ayres, of the ship *Mercury*, took twelve from the Columbia river in this manner, but while bearing down the coast, seven of them seized the whale-boat and ran from the ship; only one, however, arrived at the river. This Captain Ayres was so oppressive that three of his men left him, and were kept by Com Comley for twelve months; they afterwards got off in the American ship *Albatross*.

The chief articles of trade given in exchange to all the natives on the coast are muskets, blankets, powder, shot, red paint, (which they use to paint their faces,) tobacco, beads, buttons, thick brass wire, with which they make bracelets, rings, etc.; ready-made clothes are in great demand; but, in fact, any trifling toys will please them. The country is full of bears, wolves, tiger-cats, foxes, racoons, rabbits, muskrats, wood-rats, deer, elk, land otter, beaver, and many other animals. The sea otters are taken on the coast, but never enter the river. The war canoes are hewn out of a tree, generally the same length as the others, and the same breadth; fore and aft they have a kind of curve about 3 feet above the gunwale at each end; these curves are from 3 to 4 feet wide, and in them are a sort of loop-holes, through which they shoot their arrows in perfect safety.

What surprises the Indians very much is, that the people who come here in ships should know those who came overland; and that those who travel across the country should return again in ships.

It may be remembered, we left the river on the 10th day of January, 1817, for the Sandwich Islands, our object was, to refit the brig and cure pork. We were also to bring as many of the Sandwich Islanders to the Columbia river as we could conveniently accommodate. On the 27th we saw Owhyhee (Hawaii), after a quick and pleasant passage; we stood along shore as usual; the natives came off in great numbers, bringing pigs, tarrow, yams, goats, plantains, rope, and fruit of every description. Next day we anchored off Tyroa (Kailua), close to the king's morai (temple). King Tameameah (Kamehameha) and his family came on board as usual, and were rejoiced to see us. He assured us we should have every thing we wished for that the islands afforded or he could command; and commenced sending hogs on board.

On the 1st of February we sailed from Owhyhee (Hawaii), his majesty sending a trusty man with us named Kenopoo, to see that we got what we wanted. We had directions to touch at Mowee (Maui), where we should have plenty of hogs, salt and rope. When weighing our anchor we found it was fast under a rock, where it inevitably must have remained, had not the king sent his divers down to clear it. The depth of water was eight fathoms. We now made sail towards Mowee, our ship, as usual, full of natives. Next morning we passed Morokenee (Molokini), and made sail up Mackerey (Maalaea) bay; here we lay until the 6th, and took on board a great quantity of hogs, salt, and vegetables. This bay is very deep and wide, and nearly divides the island, there being but a narrow neck of land and very low, keeping the two parts of the island together. There is good anchorage; and the only danger arises from the trade winds, which blow so strong at times as to drive ships out of the bay with two anchors down; it lies N. E. and S. W. and is well sheltered from every other wind. The neck of land is so low, and the land so high on each side, that the N. E. trade comes through like a hurricane. On this neck of land are their principal salt-pans, where they make most excellent salt. Our next station was in Lehina (Lahaina) roads. This beautiful village has the appearance of a fine garden, laid out with the greatest taste in fish-ponds, tarrow (kalo) patches, cane patches, groves of bread fruit and plantain trees, so delightfully arranged that nothing can surpass it.

On the 9th, the brig, full of hogs and natives, got under weigh from this romantic spot, bound for Woahoo (Oahu); we were becalmed for three days between the islands of Mowee (Maui), Morotoi (Molokai), Tahoorooa (Kahoolawe), and Raini (Lanai). On the 13th of February we were off the harbour of Honorora (Honolulu), and John Harbottle, the king's pilot, came on board; but it was not till the 20th that the trade wind suffered us to get in shore. We found a brig and a ship here belonging to the king, the former was called the *Forester*, now *Taamano* (Kaahumanu), after the king's favorite wife, and had been sold to him by Captain Piggot; the ship was an American, called the *Albatross*, sold by Captain Winship. The *Taamano* (Kaahumanu) was fitting out for Canton, and taking sandal wood on board for the China market; she was commanded by Mr. Adams, the man who had navigated the *Forester* under Captain Piggot, and the crew consisted of about ten natives and ten white men. She sailed for Canton on the 22nd of February, 1817.

To our great surprise we found a very fine battery, built on the point, mounting about 60 guns, and learned that, during our absence, the Russians had sent two ships from New Archangel, or Norfolk Sound, to these islands, with Russians and Kodiacks, to form an establishment. They called at Owhyhee (Hawaii), and thence came down to Woahoo, where they were well treated by the natives, and allowed to land what they pleased; as soon as they got footing on shore, they commenced building block houses, and squaring out a place for a fort, under the direction of Mr. Shefham. They even hoisted the Russian colours. Mr. John Young, the white man before mentioned in this narrative, who had resided on these islands about 36 years, communicated this intelligence to the king and chiefs, all of whom were on Owhyhee. The chiefs were immediately sent down to Woahoo with orders from Tameameah (Kamehameha) that the Russians should quit the islands instantly, and if they did not depart quietly that force must be used. The Russians not finding themselves strong enough to resist went peaceably off. The Islanders then built the fort under the direction of John Young. A party was kept constantly on shore curing the pork, which was done in the following manner:—We killed the pigs late in the evening, bled them well, and hung them up in the tent; next morning, before sunrise, we cut them up in four-pound pieces, and took out the back-bone; the pieces were then well rubbed with salt, and packed in a puncheon, with holes in the lower head for the pickle to drain off; they remained in this manner till the next day, under a good press; they were then taken out, resalted, and packed in another cask, where they remained for a week; at the end of which they were finally packed and pickled, putting a small quantity of salt-petre in each cask; in this manner we even salted the heads; we cured about one hundred barrels and never lost a piece. While we lay here we gave half the people leave to go on shore each night; our carpenter had frequent occasion to go into the woods to cut timber, which he did in safety, and we were extremely well treated by the natives. On the 14th of April, being complete in provisions, repairs, etc., we took on board 60 natives (being all we could conveniently accommodate), for the Columbia River, and stood out of the harbour, after saluting the fort, which was returned. Made sail toward Atooi; on the 16th we got off the village of Whymea (Waimea), and were surprised at not seeing any of the natives push off. Doctor Shefham, the Russian, came on board in a bodarkee; he would not allow us to have any communication with the shore, and through policy we did not press the point, but made all sail to the northward towards Norfolk Sound. Next day we passed Mokoo Manoo, (Moku Manu) or Bird Island. There are no inhabitants here, although the land seems good, and covered with cocoanut and plantain trees. The latitude is 23° 8′ North, Longitude 161° 45 West. Arrived at Norfolk Sound on the 10th of May, and found the American brig *Brutus*, Captain Meeks, chartered by the Governor Baranoff to go to Kamschatka with a cargo of furs, and bring Russians from thence to Norfolk Sound. Finding our boarding defences of no use we sold them to the governor, who had them fixed round his house. While here we were well supplied with fish, and often visited by the natives, who brought off plenty of sea otter skins in the night; they are much the same as the Indians on the Columbia, the only difference is in the appearance of the women, who perforate their lower lip with a copper wire, enlarging the hole daily by putting in a small plug of wood, which is exchanged each day for a larger, till they get a piece of wood in of an oval shape, about two inches long, an inch broad, and half an inch thick; this drags the lip down, and leaves the gums and teeth quite bare, and gives them a most disgusting appearance. Both men and women chew tobacco, of which the women in particular are very fond. Some of the natives in Chatham Straits squeeze their heads into a sugar-loaf shape, by means of binding it round with kelp or sea weed when they are young. They also use paint, and powder their hair with the down of geese or swans. They wear the hair long, but, on the death of a chief, cut it short round the head. They have their noses perforated with a large quill. The natives here are great warriors, and very hostile to the Russians, whom they often annoy by attacking their bodarkees; however, they do not always kill them, but are satisfied with running a spear through them and leaving them to their fate.

CHAPTER VIII.

CAPE EDGECOMBE is in latitude 57° 2'
North, and longitude 135° 34' West, and is
a remarkably high bluff cape, with a mountain just above it, called Mount Edgecombe,
from which it takes its name. It has been a burning mountain, and is quite flat on the top, which is
constantly covered with snow. Ships bound to this
sound, from the southward, and coming in by
point Woodhouse, which is the south point of the
sound, must not approach nearer the point than
three miles, as there is a sunken rock on which

the sea sometimes breaks, and is very dangerous, the course from here to the light-house is north, which will take you clear of all dangers. The Russians never keep a light in the light-house, unless they see a ship in the offing before dark. The sound is full of islands, and on the south side there are some hot springs. The gun-boats are continually going round it to protect the hunters and fishermen; to carry in any canoes they may find with furs, and make prisoners of the men till they are ransomed by their friends. Whenever we arrived or sailed, we had several of the Russian boats about us to prevent the Indians from coming off to trade; but sometimes in the night they contrived to elude their vigilance, and get on board to traffic with us. We had variable winds and bad weather all the passage to the river, where we at length arrived, June 12, 1817, and came-to under the fort in our old berth, sent the islanders on shore, and commenced landing our cargo. July 12, after, as usual, completing our wood and water, we took some goods on board for the southward, and sailed to see what we could do in the way of trade with the Indians on New Albion. The American brig *Alexander* arrived here from America with stores for the settlement. She took on board the furs for Canton, and ran out of the river in company with us. We parted outside; they stood to the northward and we to the southward along shore; the weather being foggy, we sounded occasionally in from 30 to 13 fathoms water, over a bed of rocks, off Cape Foulweather, in latitude 44°

49' North, longitude 123° 56' West. On the 14th
it cleared up, and we saw Cape Orford, bearing
S. E. seven leagues; the nearest land two miles,
latitude 43° North; observed many smokes on
shore. About noon, several canoes came off
within hail of the ship; we waved to them to come
closer, which they did, displaying green boughs
and bunches of white feathers; they stopped
paddling, and one man, whom we took to be a
chief, stood up, and made a long speech, which
we did not understand. We then waved a white
flag, and they immediately pulled for the ship,
singing all the way. When they came alongside
we gave them a rope, and made signs for them to
come on board, which nothing could induce them
to do; they seemed quite terrified, and after
handing some land-furs on board, for which we
gave them beads and knives, they seemed well
pleased, and made signs that if we came nearer
the shore, they would bring us plenty. They
also brought some berries, fish, and handsome
baskets for sale. These men were tall and well
formed, their garments made of dressed deer-
skins, with a small round hat, in shape of a basin,
that fitted close round the head; none of the
women made their appearance. Their canoes
do not seem to be so well constructed as the
canoes in the Columbia, which cannot be occa-
sioned by want of material, as the country appears
to be well wooded. We observed a bay which
looked well sheltered from the N. W. winds.
About four o'clock the natives left the ship singing, and, when they got to a certain distance,
made another long speech.

We now stood along shore toward Cape Orford, sounding occasionally in from 30 to 70 fathoms; sandy bottom from four to six miles from shore; the wind increasing from N. W. stood off from the land under easy sail for the night. Next morning we ran in, and lay-to off an Indian village, to the southward of Cape Orford; saw many natives on the shore, but it blew too hard for them to launch their canoes; we intended to have anchored here, there being, apparently, a snug, well-sheltered bay, from all but the S. W., but it was too rough to send the boat from the ship to sound it; we therefore filled and ran along shore, at the distance of three miles. The land had a very fine appearance, the hills well wooded, and the plains covered with Indian huts. Towards night, the gale increased so much, that we were obliged to haul off under a close reefed main top-sail and fore-sail, and, before morning, had to lay-to under bare poles. On the 19th of July, the gale broke; we again stood in for the land, and were becalmed for three days, within six miles of the shore, where we saw many smokes. We were driven fast to the southward by the current; on the 24th a breeze sprang up, and we made sail for Port Trinidad, in latitude 41° 3', longitude 123° 54' west; hauled into a small sandy bay, where we moored, sheltered from all winds, a few ships' lengths from the shore, in nine fathoms sandy bottom. This bay is full of high rocks, which are always covered with birds, and round it are scattered many Indian villages. We had scarcely time to moor before we were surrounded with canoes; we triced our boarding nets up, and shut all our ports but one, at which the natives entered, keeping all the canoes on the starboard side; and, as the Indians came on board, we took their bows and daggers from them, at which they seemed much displeased. One man (a chief) would not give up his dagger, and we pushed him back into his canoe; upon which he immediately strung his bow, and pointed an arrow at me, as being the most active in sending him out of the ship. In an instant he had several muskets pointed at him, upon seeing which, he lost no time in laying his bow down. Shortly after he came on board, and seemed sorry for what he had done, and made me a present of a fine bow. Everything being thus settled, we gave them some bread and molasses, of which they eat heartily. We then commenced trading, and got a few land furs, which they brought off, for pieces of iron-hoop, cut into 6-inch lengths. They also brought us plenty of red deer and berries. In the afternoon, some women made their appearance: the people offered them blankets and axes, but nothing could tempt them to come on board. This is the only place on the coast where we could not induce the females to visit the ship. It appears that these natives have not had much communication with Europeans, as they do not know the use of fire-arms; nor have they any iron among them. Their daggers are made of a sort of flint-stone, and they are clothed in dressed leather apparel, prettily ornamented with shells. The women wear a very finely dressed leather petticoat, which reaches half way down the leg, and a square garment of the same thrown loosely over the shoulders. Their tongues and chins are tattooed; the former is quite black, the latter in stripes. Whether this is considered a mark of beauty or not-I cannot tell, but the women here are in general very handsome and well made. We saw a cross on shore, fixed there by the Spaniards many years ago, when there was a Spanish launch driven on shore, and the Indians massacred the whole crew. The different tribes in this bay are always at war with each other; they never met on board, and if the tribe which was on board trading, saw another tribe approaching, they immediately went on shore to protect their wives and property. They all seem to be brave, warlike people. Their canoes are by far the safest I ever saw on the coast, being from 16 to 20 feet long, and from 6 to 8 feet broad, square at both ends and flat bottomed. They have ridges inside about a foot apart, which look exactly like the timbers of a boat, and serve to strengthen them very much. The only words of this tongue we could pick up was. *I ai guai*, which is a term of friendship, and *chilese*, which means barter. When they speak they put the tongue to the roof of the mouth, and utter sounds as if their mouth were full. After having bought all the furs here, on the 24th of July we weighed anchor, and, after encountering considerable difficulties, owing to the bad weather, succeeded in getting out. This was fortunate, as, had we gone on shore, (there not being the least shelter in this part of the bay),

166

the Indians were ready to receive and massacre us, for they are, without exception, the most savage tribes on all the coast.

Having stood out to sea, we deepened our water to 45 fathoms, when the wind again died away, the sea setting us fast on to the shore; we had but one bower anchor and stream left, and, to crown all, it came on a thick fog. We spent a most anxious night, sounding from 40 to 20 fathoms. We could hear the sea break on the beach very distinctly; the order was given to stand by our best bower anchor, when it pleased God to send a fine breeze from the N. W. and deliver us from our dangerous situation. We immediately made all sail from the coast. Next day, July 26, we saw Cape Mendocino, (latitude 40° 19' north, longitude 124° 7' west), north about four leagues, found our bowsprit sprung, and determined to run to Bodago-bay and fish it; stood along shore accordingly, and on the 28th got off the settlement, fired a gun, and several bodarkees came off, bringing with them some fresh pork and vegetables. We here moored and fished our bowsprit. Captain Jennings then went to the settlement in the whale boat to try and dispose of his cargo to the Russians, but returned to the ship in two days without having effected his purpose. While we lay here the Russians sent us some fresh provision and vegetables; the natives also visited us in their canoes, which are nothing more than several large bundles of rushes lashed together. They seem to be the poorest tribe in these parts, although the country is by far the finest; the climate is so pure and the grounds so good, that the Russians grow two crops per year.

The Russian establishment on the coast of New Albion is in latitude 38° 30' and longitude —° —', about four leagues to the northward of this fine bay and harbour, called Bodago, where they have a large store. Here their ships generally call and sometimes winter, there being no shelter for ships off the establishment. The reason for their having it so far from the harbour is the scarcity of timber, which is very necessary in the forming of a settlement, and where they now are, the country is covered with fine oak, ash, and pine timber, fit for ship building. They had on the stocks, and nearly fit for launching, a fine brig of 150 tons, built of good oak. They get excellent hemp on the coast of California, and make good rope. This settlement consists of about 100 houses and huts, with a small fort on the point, and about 500 inhabitants, Russians and Kodiacks. The land is in the highest state of cultivation, growing excellent wheat, potatoes, hemp and all kinds of vegetables; and the soil so rich as to produce (as already mentioned) two crops in the year. I have seen radishes that weighed from one pound to 28 pounds, and much thicker than a stout man's thigh, and quite good all through, without being the least spongy. They have a large stock of cattle, sheep, and pigs; and seem to be in the most flourishing condition under the direction of Governor Kutzkoff. Hence hunters are sent down the coast of California for the purpose of taking the sea otter, which are very plentiful along the coast. The colony also sends a vessel to Norfolk Sound once a year, with the furs collected, and with wheat and hemp. Norfolk Sound is the principal depot; from thence the furs are sent to Kamschatka.

CHAPTER IX.

Coasting Trade to Sir F. Drake's Harbour.—Return to Trinidad Bay.—Attacked by the Indians.—Return to Columbia.—Mission up the Country to the Cladsap Tribe; its Success.—Description of the Country.—The Northwest Company's Establishment.

ON the 18th of August, 1817, we completed our work here, (Bodago), weighed the anchor, and stood away for the Farelone rocks of islands, in the latitude of 37° 40' North, and longitude 122° 20' West. Next day we ran close to the rocks, and I went on shore to look for fur-seals. On landing we found plenty of hair seals, but very few fur; we knocked down a few of them, and brought them on board, with a number of young gulls, which were fat and good. We then made sail towards a larger group of islands, where also we landed, and were surprised to find about thirty Russians and Kodiacks with their wives. They had a flag-staff erected, but showed no colours. Their houses were built of stone, and they seemed very comfortable; they remain here for the purpose of collecting fur-seals and drying the flesh of the sea-lion, which is quite as good as Spanish jerked beef. In fine weather, a skin-boat comes from Bodago with a supply of fresh water, there not being a drop on the islands, and, in return, takes what meat and skins have been collected. The people have no means of leaving the island, having no boat, nor materials to build one. Finding we could do nothing here, we took on board a good stock of seals and gull's eggs, also plenty of young gulls, We then stood for the harbour of Sir Francis Drake, and next day anchored in the bay in 5½ fathoms, hoisted the boats out, and I went with a party on shore to look for natives. I returned on board in the evening, having seen but few, and those very poor. This part of the country is delightfully pleasant, with many small rivers running through the valleys. While on shore, we killed a number of large snakes and adders, and saw many deer and foxes, but they were very shy. We also observed the tracks of bears. This bay is very well sheltered from all winds. August 10th, 1817, we ran along shore to the northward; passed many Indian villages, but no natives came off, I believe for want of canoes, there being no wood on this part of the coast. On the 20th of August, we again stood into the bay of Trinidad, to endeavour to receive our anchor, and next morning I went with the whale boat and long-boat with purchases to raise it, leaving the captain with only six men on board to take care of the ship. We started before daylight, that the natives should not take notice of us; it came on so thick a fog, that we not only did not succeed in finding the buoy, but had much difficulty in regaining the vessel. About six o'clock in the evening, however, we got on board, and learnt that the Indians had been very troublesome during our absence. In consequence of their seeing but few men, they had made several attempts to board the ship, but were as often beat out of the nets. It was of no use to point the muskets at them, for they were ignorant of their effect, until some of the men shot several gulls that were flying about the ship. Upon this, they began to be less daring, and, as we fired a few muskets on approaching, they made for the shore, as quick as possible. We now gave up all hopes of recovering our anchor, and at daylight weighed, and made sail, thinking it dangerous to remain any longer among this savage tribe. We stood along shore to the N. E., saw many small villages, but the sea was so rough that none of the natives came off. Next day we stood close under Point St. George to find anchorage, seeing a very large village and many natives on the shore. We sounded round the bay in from 12 to 20 fathoms, over a foul bottom, one and two miles from shore. Many canoes came off, and the natives appeared quite friendly. We bought several good sea otter skins at an axe for each skin; many bows, arrows, daggers, etc., for small beads. The canoes here are similar to those at Port Trinidad. As the anchorage was not good, and we had bought all the furs brought off, we stood out to sea; the natives kept on board as long as they could. We then beat up along shore to the northward, trading with the Indians, to Point Gregory, in latitude 43°. Here we continued our traffic, and on the 2nd of September hauled off to the westward, to look for a seal island, said to have been seen by an American vessel. On the 10th of October, after a fruitless search, we arrived off the Columbia river, sent the furs on shore, and set the carpenter to work to make a bowsprit; we took on board wood and water; also six long 12-pounders, with powder and shot, for the Sandwich Islands. On the 20th of October, I was sent with a party of thirty-three from the fort and ship to the Cladsaps' winter quarters, about 30 miles distant, to bring back John Carpenter, the blacksmith, (one of the men we landed here on our first arrival); he had behaved very well for some time, but at length got quite unruly, and deserted to the Cladsap tribe. Several messengers were sent at different times, but to no purpose, as he was protected by the tribe, none of whom had visited the fort since his desertion. Mr. Keith, the governor, fearing that the Indians would make an attempt to storm the fort at some time, headed by this desperate man, determined to have him banished from the river; and I was accordingly dispatched with orders to bring him dead or alive, together with the chief of the village at which I found him. We left the ship at about 6 o'clock in the evening in the cutter and whale boat, and pulled up Young's River to the south point, where we landed, and secured the boats in a small creek, and left two men to take care of them. We travelled through woods, over

173

plains, crossed small rivers and creeks, passed many Indian habitations, and just at day-light arrived at the winter village of the Cladsaps, before the Indians were awake. We sent one of our guides into the chief's huts to see if Carpenter was there, who returned in a few minutes, and informed us that he was, and asleep; I then placed the men round the house to prevent his escape, and taking the second mate with me, we entered the hut, found him in bed, and, after a violent struggle, secured him, by lashing his hands behind him. By this time the Indians were collecting and arming. They poured in from all parts, and seemed disposed to prevent our taking away our prisoner; and Carpenter's female companion was very active in instigating them to liberate her husband. I drew my party up in a double line, and then stepped out and told the Indians, that I did not come to trouble them, but merely to take the white man to the fort. They answered, that he came to them for protection, and they would protect him. I informed them, if they attempted to stop him, what they might expect; and ordered the party to march, which it did without being molested. I did not like to provoke a quarrel with them by taking their chief, there being about 156 men well armed with bows and muskets, who might have cut us all off, before we could reach our boats. We therefore took Carpenter, and with him made the best of our way, passing over a most beautiful country, an extensive plain, with many small rivulets. This spot appeared capable of the highest cultivation, and was covered with berrie of different sorts. We saw many horses and deer, and also the mountain sheep. There were many small villages scattered about the plain, the natives of which treated us very kindly. In the evening we arrived at the boats, and about 8 o'clock at the fort, all very much fatigued with our journey, the result of which gave great satisfaction to the governor. Carpenter was well secured over the gate of the fort; his hand-cuffs were made with a nut to screw tight on, and then clinched; his legs were fastened in the same manner, and a large hoop made to go tight round his body, with a chain from each side of it, which was stretched tight out, and locked to the post of the gate. Here he was kept until the *Columbia* was ready for sea. November the 14th we left the river for the Sandwich Islands, to sell the vessel; and if we did not succeed at the Islands, we had orders to proceed to Norfolk Sound, and dispose of her to the Russians. The Northwest Company's Establishment lies about seven miles from Point Adam, on the south side of the river, above a small bay, where ships are in great safety out of the strength of the tide. There is a very good wharf with a crane for landing or shipping goods. The settlement is a square of about 200 yards, surrounded by pickets about 15 feet high, and protected by two bastions, one on the S. W. and the other on the N. E. corner. Each of these bastions mounts eight guns, four and six pounders; and there are loop-holes for musketry. The grand entrance is through a large double gate on the north side, above which there is a platform for the sentry to walk; on this are several swivels mounted. As you enter the fort, or square, there is a two-story house, with two long 18-pounders in front of it on the south side; on the east is a range of low buildings, where the clerks have their apartments; and in the same row stands the grand hall, where the gentlemen assemble to dinner, etc. The houses for the men are on the same side, and behind the two-story or governor's house; in the S. W. corner, is the magazine well secured; along the west side stands a range of stores, tailor's shop, and Indian trading shop; in the S. E. corner the blacksmith's and cooper's shops, and on the N. E. corner a granary for the corn. In the N. W. corner stands a very high flag-staff, erected by the crew of the *Columbia*. The whole of the settlers here do not exceed 150 men, most of whom keep Indian women, who live inside of the fort with them. Nearly all the settlers are Canadians. The clerks and partners are Scotch. They are constantly employed in cutting down the wood, and improving the fort: the men are not allowed the ground on their own account, the company being fearful they would in time become independent, and leave them. The Company's canoes arrive here from the interior, in the spring and fall; they bring the furs that are collected at the different posts on the west side of the stoney mountains, and take back stores for the posts. The canoes are manned with Euroque Indians and Canadians, under the direction of a partner and several young clerks. When they arrive in the fall, the boatmen encamp outside the fort; they are each served out with a half pint of rum, and their year's clothing, and orders are issued, that those men who do not get drunk, must go to the wood and cut timber. The liquor shop is then opened, and kept by one of the clerks; a scene of drunkenness and all manner of vice follows. A frolick of this kind will cost them a year's pay and upwards; they generally agree for two years, at the end of which time they find themselves in debt, are therefore obliged to agree for two years longer, and in this manner are kept in the service till they are gray-headed. The Company have a train of posts from the Columbia River to the rocky or stoney mountains, and from thence to Montreal; all the furs that are collected at the west side of these mountains are brought to the Columbia, and sent from thence to China; and all that are collected on the east side are sent to Montreal, and from thence to England. At this settlement they have cleared about 200 acres of ground, and planted about 20 acres with potatoes for the use of the gentlemen, their object being to collect furs, and not to cultivate or improve the land. They have about twelve head of cattle with some pigs and goats, imported here from California; their stock does not increase, for want of proper care, the wolves often carrying off goats and pigs.

177

CHAPTER X.

Voyage to the Sandwich Islands; various Transactions there; Superstitious Omen; Death of a Chief; Remarkable Funeral Ceremonies, Taboo, and Customs connected with these Rites.—Whymea.—The Russian Intrigues with the Natives, and their consequences.—Different trading trips, to show the Nature of the Island Commerce.—The ship given up.—Situation of the Men on shore.

OUR passage to the Sandwich Islands was quick and pleasant. On the 6th of December we made Owhyhee, stood along shore towards Toyhoy (Kawaihae) bay, and ran in. Finding no natives came off, we sent the whale boat on shore to know what was the reason. The boat soon returned with an account that the natives were celebrating their annual festival, called muckka-hitee (makahiki). This festival lasts a month, during which time a canoe is not allowed to go on salt water. We also heard, that king Tameahmeah was then at the village of Tyroa, his favourite residence; we made all sail for that place, where we arrived on the 10th, and

178

came too with our only bower anchor off the Morai. No canoes being allowed to come off, Captain Jennings went on shore to see the king; in the evening the boat returned with some hogs and tarrow. The king Tameahmeah told Captain Jennings if he would go to the Island of Woahoo, and remain until the muckka-hitee was over, he should be then able to agree with him about the purchase of the ship. We accordingly left Tyroa; when we got our anchor up, we found one arm broken off. We made all sail for Woahoo, and on the 14th arrived off the harbour. Captain Jennings went on shore, and sent off an anchor. We then came too outside the reef, in 14 fathoms over a sandy bottom, and on the 18th we got into the harbour. We found the king's brig had returned from Canton, and was laid up We found here the brig *Bordeaux Packet*, which had been purchased from the Americans about a month before. A large ship, called the *Myrtle*, was condemned by the Russians, and hauled on shore. We moored close to the shore and saluted the fort, which was returned by them. In the night it came on to blow very hard from the N.E., and continued for several days.

We sent John Carpenter on shore, and discharged him of the crew. The taboo was still on, consequently none of the natives came on board. On the 24th of December, the muckkahitee being over, the king's prime minister, named Kreymokoo (Kalaimoku), commonly called Pitt, came on board with all the chiefs, accompanied by John Young, to inspect the vessel, previous to their

purchasing of her. They seemed much astonished at our large battery guns; we got one on
deck, and, mounting it,, fired several rounds of
shot, at which the chiefs were much pleased,
and the natives crowded from all parts of the
island to see the poo'nu'ee (pu nui), as they call
a great gun. They were all very particular in
measuring its length, breadth, and size of the
bore. After the chiefs had carefully inspected
every part of the brig, John Young was asked
his opinion of her. He told Mr. Pitt she would
answer their purpose very well. Kreymokoo
upon this agreed to give twice the full of the
vessel of sandal wood for her, to be delivered in
a space of time not exceeding six months, and
that we should hold possession of the vessel till
all the wood was delivered, and that we were to
be found in provisions while we remained on the
island. An agreement was drawn up and signed
by Captain Jennings and Kreymokoo. The
next day being Christmas day, we invited all the
chiefs and respectable white men on the island to
dine with us on shore; we spent a most pleasant
day, and the chiefs remained with us to a late
hour. We had a dinner cooked apart for the
chiefs' wives, as they were not allowed to eat
with the men. Next day we took on board the
king's taxes, and January 11th, 1818, we sailed
for Owhyhee, the brig loaded with provisions
and cloth of the country, this being the time
at which the natives pay their half-year's taxes.
We had also a number of chiefs on board,
and about 400 natives, men, women, and children.

There was scarcely room to move on the decks or in the cabin; even the chains, tops and bowsprit were crowded with them. We touched at Mowee, where they all landed for a few days, and nothing went forward but feasting and rejoicing. On the 16th, the chiefs again came on board, and we got under weigh for Owhyhee, the ship, as before, full of natives. In crossing the channel, between Mowee and Owhyhee, we were near upsetting the vessel, being top heavy, from the number of them on deck and about the rigging. On the 18th, we anchored off Tyroa, and Tameameah came on bord. On his approach, all the natives jumped overboard, and left us clear decks. We commenced firing a salute, when the king called out to us, in a pleasant tone, to stop, as the powder was now his, and he wanted it for other purposes, probably for the Russians, if they should come to trouble him. He was delighted with the large guns; and the natives came on board, as at Woahoo, to see the poo'nu'ee. Their fame was soon spread over the island, but the next day we landed them, and by that means got rid of the curious natives; they were placed in a square in front of the royal residence, where thousands of the people were daily collected to look at them. Tameameah found one fault with them, which was, that they took too much powder, (a charge being four pounds), but he took all our small arms, powder, and everything he thought would be useful to him, and made the brig over to his son and heir Rieo Rieo (Liholiho). On the 26th of January, we sailed from Owhyhee towards

Mowee, with our usual cargo of natives; next day we anchored in Lehina Roads, and took on board the king's taxes, and made sail for Woahoo. In our passage down, during the night, a star shot very vividly—the natives gave a sudden scream, and told us that the star shooting foretold the death of an Owhyhee chief. On the first of February we arrived at Woahoo; in crossing the reef the brig took the ground, but was soon lightened by the natives jumping overboard and swimming on shore. About a week after our arrival, a chief, named Tereacoo (Kaleioku) died suddenly; he went to bed well over night, and in the morning got up, and according to custom, smoked a pipe, after which he lay down and died. All the natives were immediately tabooed, or prohibited from going on the water; they all appeared to be in great grief, crying and making a dreadful noise. They commenced knocking out they teeth, cutting off their hair, and burning their flesh with the bark of a tree; both men and women going about quite naked, to demonstrate their grief.

On the death of the chief, the priests assembled; they fenced the house in for about fifty yards square with wands, having white flags flying on them. None of the natives dare come inside this fence, though several thousands of them were collected round it. There was a large fire made on the outside of the house and inside of the fence or prohibited space; the priests then began cutting up the body. They brought the heart out, and set it in the fire, praying very devoutly while it was burning; after which they

182

collected the ashes, put them into a calabash, or gourd, slung it to a pole, and spread a beautiful feather cloak over it. Then two of the chiefs, Hikanees, or confidential men, took the pole on their shoulders, and ran towards the water, crying out very loud, "Noho, noho!" (which means sit or lie down;) as these men passed, all the natives lay down and stripped themselves. They walked up to their middle in water, and deposited the ashes; afterwards the liver and all the inside were treated in the same manner. At *sundown* this part of the ceremony ceased, and a crier went round the village, calling out, that if any man, woman, or child, were seen out of their houses, or showed a light or fire, or even smoked a pipe, after 8 o'clock that evening, they would instantly be put to death. These restrictions extended not only to the white people, but even to the ships in the harbour; nay, hogs, dogs, fowls, etc., were not allowed to be out, least they should make a noise, nor were the ships suffered to strike the bells next morning.

At sunrise the Taboo was taken off the ships, but still remained in force on shore. This day the priests were employed burning the flesh off the bones, and scraping them quite clean; the ashes were deposited in the sea; the bones were then carefully packed up, and a large double canoe dispatched with them to Owhyhee. Six hours after the canoe sailed, the Taboo was taken off the bay, and canoes were allowed to go on the water;—in this manner they employ ceremonies towards all the people of rank. The common people dig up the bones of their relatives after the flesh is rotted from them, scrape and clean them well, wrap them up in cloth, put them into calabashes, or gourds, and hang them up in their houses.

We lay in the harbour until the 17th of March, 1818, without anything particular occuring, until that day, when we received orders from Tameameah to proceed to the island of Atooai (Kauai) for a cargo of sandal-wood. Teymotoo, or Cox, with several other chiefs, came on board. We made sail, and on the following day came too in Whymea Roads. One mile from the village, the English ensign was displayed on a very fine fort, mounting about thirty guns; the natives came off in great numbers; they informed us that the Russians had built the fort, in which there were dungeons, and had actually gone so far as to confine some white men and natives. The Russians advised Tamoree (Kaumualii), king of Atooai, to shake off Tameameah's yoke, and declare war against him, in which they would assist him; they made him a present of a schooner, and he gave them in return a large tract of land. Tama'honreeranee (Kamahalolani), the head chief under Tamooree, was averse to these proceedings. The Russians wished to send Tamooree to Petersburg, but could never get him on board. At length Tamooree discovered that they wished to possess themselves of the island; he consulted with his chiefs, returned their schooner, (which they refused,) and ordered them on board their ships, three of which were lying in a snug harbour* at the west end of the island. They resisted, and a scuffle ensued, in which three Russians and several natives were killed, but the latter at last forced them on board, and Doctor Shefham made his escape to Canton in an American vessel. The Russian ships went to Norfolk Sound. The fort does great credit to the engineer; it is situate on a high point at the entrance of the river, and protects the whole town. The king, chiefs, and about 150 warriors live within it, and keep a regular guard; they have a number of white men for the purpose of working the guns, etc.

Our chiefs landed, and were well received by Tamooree; and the next morning they commenced sending wood on board. About 500 canoes were employed in bringing it off, and by the 25th of March we had the ship quite full. The king behaved extremely well, and sent us off plenty of hogs and vegetables. Our chiefs came on board, as did also some Atooi chiefs. We weighed and made sail for Woahoo, where we anchored the next day, landed our wood, and lay until the 19th, when we took on board a cargo of salt for the west end of Woahoo. Next day we sailed for Whymea bay, on the west end of the island, to get another cargo of wood. In our passage we touched at Wyeni (Waianae), and took on board some wood and hogs. We lay here for a few days, and then sailed along shore for Whymea, where we arrived on the 22rd, threw our ballast out, and took on board a full

* Refers to Hanalei.

185

cargo of wood in thirty-six hours—more than 200 canoes employed in bringing it off, day and night. We weighed and made sail for Honororoa, where we arrived on the 28th, and sent the wood on shore. On the 1st of May, 1818, we had all our wood on shore and stored. On the 2nd of May, we hauled down the English colours, and hoisted the island colours, saluting them with seven guns; we then gave the ship up to Kreymokoo, or Pitt, and went on shore to the houses prepared for our reception. It was with the greatest regret I left the ship, for it seemed as if I had lost my home; and in fact it was some time before I felt myself at all comfortable. I had sailed on board the *Columbia* from August, 1813, to May, 1818, a period of nearly five years; when she left England, the crew consisted of twenty-five persons, and when we sold the vessel at these islands, the steward and a black man (who had been for several years with me in the West Indian trade) and myself were all that remained, and even these left before the vessel was given up. Our houses were the largest and most pleasantly situated of any in the village, and fronting the harbour: (they were built by four different villages, each taking a house to build and furnish), and quite finished in three days. They consisted of two sleeping houses and two eating houses, (the one for women and the other for men); the sleeping-houses and women's eating-house were surrounded by a fence fifty yards square; the men's eating-house was outside of this fence, but fenced in in like manner, with a door that led from the sleeping-house fence to it. The houses are built in the following manner; they begin by driving stakes in the ground eight feet high and three feet apart, forked at the upper ends, in which forks are laid handsome straight poles; the ridge pole is raised by temporary stakes, the rafters are forked at the lower ends, which rest on the forks of the upright; the upper ends of the rafters cross each other on the ridge-pole, and are well lashed to it; a second ridge pole is now placed in the cross of the rafters above the first one, to which it is well lashed; they then tie on neat twigs or canes, in the manner of laths, and thatch the house all over with dry grass or leaves of the tee-root. There was a door and two windows in the end. The interiors were beat down quite hard, and a quantity of rushes strewed smooth, and well covered with a large coarse mat, made the size of the house, above which others were laid of a finer quality. At one end was built a large bed-place, stuffed with dry grass, and covered neatly with mats. Along each side were built sofas, stuffed and covered the same as the bed, to keep which out of sight there was a light partition. In front of the house was built a raini (lanai), or shed, covered with the branches of cocoanut trees, and here also a sofa was built. The square in front of the house was strewed each morning with green rushes. We had a man from Tameameah who acted as steward, and whose business it was to find us in everything we wanted. We had also a watchman to walk round the houses at night, to give the alarm of fire, which happens frequently.

CHAPTER XI.

*The Sandwich Islands.—A Patriot or Runaway Ship.
—History of its change of Masters, Piracies and
Plundering.*

ABOUT the middle of May, the *Columbia* took a cargo to Owhyhee. Captain Jennings went in her to give her up to the King, leaving me to take care of the wood while he was Owhyhee. Several American ships called here from the coast of Chili, bound to Canton, in which most of our crew got off; at this time a a canoe arrived from Owhyhee, with an account of a large fighting ship having come to Owhyhee full of men, but of what country they could not tell. A few days after May 20th, 1818, one of the King's vessels made her appearance from that island, and informed us that a patriot ship, called the *Santa Rosa*, had arrived from the coast of Peru, under the command of Captain Turner, from whom Tameameah had purchased the ship and cargo, for 6000 piculs of sandal wood. It struck me very forcibly, that she must be some ship with which the crew had run away, or they could not afford to sell her for 6000 piculs, as she had a very valuable cargo of dry goods on board, and a great deal of money, which was, however, shared among the crew. The people were on shore after they had made their bargain, and three of them came down to Woahoo in the King's vessel. I got into conversation with one of them, who was half intoxicated, and after inquiring into the particulars of their cruise, I asked him what they had done with their former Captain? By this question he was thrown off his guard, and answered, that he had been sent on shore with thirteen others, at Valparaiso. When I learned this, I went to the chief, named Bokee, and made him acquainted with the circumstance; he had them immediately brought to the fort, where an examination took place, in the course of which it came out, that the ship, *Santa Rosa*, alias *Checka Boca*, alias *Liberty*, had been fitted out at the River Plate, under the command of Captain Turner, and had sailed round Cape Horn, to cruise against the Spaniards in the North and South Pacific; on going round the Horn there were some symptons of mutiny: the men would not allow punishment to be inflicted, and Captain Turner threatened hard that he would punish them severely, when the ship arrived at Valparaiso. When they had fine weather they were in the habit of exercising the guns, and on Sunday, the 27th of July, 1817, having thus secured them, the man at the mast-head, called out '*A sail, ho!*' the people ran to their quarters, and one of the officers went aloft with the glass to look for the vessel; when the crew loaded the guns, and turned them aft, at the same time seizing the captain and officers, and crying out *Liberty!* Captain Turner was standing on the companion with a spy glass in his hand, when a man of the name of Griffiths, took him by the legs and threw him off. The first lieutenant, Mr. Coran, was in the cabin getting his pistols, when he heard the noise on deck, and found the ship in possession of the mutineers; he fired his pistols up the companion by which one man was wounded. The captain called out to him to blow the ship up; to prevent which, the sailors broke the sky-light, and got down and secured him. All the officers were then confined in irons in the forecastle, and a master's mate, named McDonald, took command of the vessel. When they got off Valparaiso, they sent the captain and officers on shore, (excepting Mr. Prockley, the master, whom they kept to navigate the ship). They then ran to the island of Juan Fernandes to water, and stood along the coast, where they captured and destroyed many Spanish vessels. Their next run was to the Galipagos Islands to refit, where a second mutiny was sent on foot, but discovered. They sent the principals on shore, one of whom was drowned in landing. Here Mr. Prockley, the master, left them, and went off in an English whale ship. Mr. McDonald then assumed the name of Turner, took the command, and appointed officers.

When the ship was fitted and watered, they again ran in for the shore, where they took towns, destroyed vessels, robbed and burnt churches; in short, they became the terror of the coast. They sent a party of forty men, under the command of Griffiths, who was the first lieutenant, to go into a port, and cut out some vessels, of which they had information; but, when this party were out of sight of the ship, it was agreed by those who remained on board, to steer her to the Sandwich Islands and sell her which they accordingly did. Upon our obtaining this information of the *Santa Rosa*, we sent an account of it to Tameameah, who gave orders for the men to be distributed among the chiefs, each to have a certain number under his charge to be answerable for; shortly after this, the party who had been away under the command of Mr. Griffiths, arrived at Owhyhee in a small brig, which they had captured. They were outrageous at finding the ship in possession of the king, and wanted him to give her up, offering him the brig and all her cargo in exchange; but he refused to do so, saying, they were robbers, and he would hold the ship for the owners. He had her accordingly hauled close in shore, and a number of white men and natives continually on board, and the guns double shotted. Mr. McDonald made his escape on board the brig; they touched at Woahoo; I went on board, and they gave me letters for England, which I since delivered. Hence they ran to Atooai and back to Woahoo, hovering about the islands for some time in hopes of regaining their ship. In the middle of June, Captain Jennings returned from Owhyhee, leaving the King in a poor state of health; and we now only awaited the arrival of American N. W. ships (which generally call here in their passage to China), to freight our wood to Canton.

CHAPTER XII.

Account of the Sandwich Islands. — Woahoo. — Customs, Etc.

THE Island of Woahoo is by far the most important of the group of the Sandwich Islands, chiefly on account of its excellent harbours and good water. It is in a high state of cultivation: and abounds with cattle, hogs, sheep, goats, horses, etc., as well as vegetables and fruit of every description. The ships in those seas generally touch at Owhyhee, and get permission from Tameameah, before they can go into the harbour of Woahoo. He sends a confidential man on board to look after the vessel, and keep the natives from stealing; and, previous to entering the harbour of Honorora (Honolulu), they must pay eighty dollars harbour duty, and twelve dollars to John Harbottle, the pilot. This duty has only lately been laid on, on account of the King's brig *Taamano*, having to pay for her anchorage at Macao, when sent there with a cargo of sandal wood, in 1816. Tameameah justly observes, that if his ships have to pay on entering a foreign port, it is but reasonable that foreign ships should pay on entering his ports. There

are three close harbours on the south side of
Woahoo, between Diamond hill and Barber's
Point. On rounding Diamond hill the village of
Wyteetee (Waikiki) appears through large groves
of cocoanut and bread-fruit trees; it has a most
beautiful appearance, the land all round in the
highest state of cultivation, and the hills covered
with wood; a beautiful plain extending as far as
the eye can reach. A reef of coral runs along
the whole course of this shore, within a quarter
of a mile of the beach, on which the sea breaks
high; inside this reef there is a passage for canoes.
Ships frequently anchor in the bay, in from sixteen to twenty fathoms, over a sand and coral
bottom. Several of the king's old vessels are
hauled upon shore and sheds built over them.
His Majesty formerly resided at this village, but of
late years has preferred his native place, Owhyhee. About four miles to the westward of Wyteetee is the village and harbour of Honorora; it
is the largest on the island, as the natives collect
from all other parts to be near the shipping. The
harbour is known by a deep and remarkable
valley over the village, through which the N. E.
trade wind blows very strong. The island is not
more than five leagues across at this part. The
best time to get into the harbour is early in the
morning, before the wind sets violently in a contrary direction; the chief generally sends a number of large double canoes to tow the ship in, as
the entrance of the harbour is not more than a
quarter of a mile wide. Small vessels, when
about to enter, run close to the east side of the

reef, where hundreds of the natives are collected, and, by throwing a rope to them, the ship is pulled up to the anchorage.—Ships can moor close to the shore, so as to have a stage from thence, and be as safe as if they were in the London Docks. A fine round battery on the S. E. flat, or point, mounting about sixty guns, protects the village and harbour. The fort occupies about eight acres of ground; the facing of the wall is stone, about eighteen feet high, and about the same breadth on the top, gradually sloping to make a base of about thirty feet. It is constructed of hard clay and dry grass and sand well cemented together; on the top of this wall are embrasures built of the same materials, without stone; the guns are mounted all round, and are from four to eighteen pounders, the heaviest guns facing the sea. The magazine is under ground and well secured; and in the middle of the fort stands a flag-staff, on which the island colours are displayed, consisting of a union jack, with a red and blue stripe for each island. Round the flag-staff are the chiefs houses, and barracks for the soldiers. The strictest discipline is observed; the guard relieved very regularly in the night, and the word "All is well," sung out in English every ten minutes ! The Americans supply them with powder and stores, for which they get sandal wood, rope, hogs, vegetables, etc. The village consists of about 300 houses regularly built, those of the chiefs being larger and fenced in. Each family must have three houses, one to sleep in, one for the men to eat in, and one for the women,—the sexes not being allowed to eat together. Cocoanut, bread-fruit, and castor-oil-nut* trees, form delicious shades, between the village and a range of mountains which runs along the island in a N. W. and S. E. direction. The ground is laid out in beautiful square patches, where the tarrow grows, round which they plant sugar canes and Indian corn. They have also a number of fine fish ponds, in which they keep mullet and a fish they call ava. On the N. W. side of the harbour is a fresh water river, where a ship's long boat can go up about two miles and fill the water casks in the boat. About three miles to westward of Honorora is a second harbour, easier of access and superior to the other in every respect, except the want of a watering place. There are but few farmers' and fishermen's houses hereabouts, and for this reason, it is not frequented; in fact few ships know any thing of it. About six miles to the westward of this harbour, is Wy Momi, or Pearl Water. This inlet extends about five leagues up the country in a northerly direction; it is about four miles across in the widest part, and at the entrance about half a mile. There is not more than fifteen feet of water on the bar or reef at high water, and inside from six to eighteen fathoms mud and sand. There is an island about two miles in circumference in the middle of this inlet, belonging to Mr. Manning (Don Marin), a Spaniard, who has been here for many years. It is covered with goats, rabbits, and hogs, belonging to him. At

---

* The writer here has reference to the kukuitree.

the head of the inlet is a run of very fine fresh water, and provisions are here cheap and plentiful. There are many divers employed here, diving for the pearl oysters, which are found in great plenty. We saved them much trouble and labor by presenting the King with an oyster dredge we had on board, with which Tameameah was highly delighted. The reef, or flat, extends from this inlet to Barber's point which is about eight miles to the westward, and from thence several miles to sea in a S. W. direction. Round Barber's Point to the north is the bay and village of Y-eni (Waianae); and a little further to the N. W. stands the village of Y-rooa (Waialua); on the west end of the island is the village and bay of Wymea. There are no harbours on the N. E. side of the island, and only two large villages. As I before observed, the women are not allowed to enter the men's eating-houses, or even to appear on the inside of the fence, on pain of death. Neither men nor women are allowed to eat in the sleeping-houses; the women are prohibited from eating pork, cocoanuts, bananas, plantains, and many other things, which are used as offering to the gods, and it is considered a profanation if a woman should touch anything so offered. They are not even allowed to touch anything that goes inside of the men's eating house; they have their own vessels to eat and drink out of; and they must have a separate fire, at which to cook their victuals; the men's fire being called yahee taboo (ahi kapu), or prohibited fire, from which they cannot even light their pipes, though both young and old are

196

very fond of smoking tobacco. There are several morais, or churches in the village, and at new moon the priests, chiefs and hikanees (aikane) enter them with offerings of hogs, plantains, and cocoanuts, which they set before the wooden images. Theplace is fenced in, and have pieces of white flags flying on the fences. They remain in the morai three nights and two days at new moon, beginning at sun-set and ending at sun-rise, feasting on roast hogs, and praying all the time. On the first quarter, they remain inside two nights and one day; full moon and last quarter, the same time. While the chiefs and priests are in the morai, the women are prohibited from going on the salt water, either in canoes or boats, or even from touching it; neither are they permitted to come within forty yards of the morai. The common people know nothing more about their religion than a stranger who never saw the islands. They pay the greatest respect to their chiefs and priests, and are kept in superstitious ignorance. Their muckahitee, or annual festival, commences in November; it begins by three of the most expert warriors throwing each a spear at Tameameah, who is obliged to stand without anything in his hand to fend them off, the first spear he catches, and with it makes the other spears fly several yards above his head. He then breaks a cocoanut; the sea is tabooed, and none of the natives are allowed to go near it. The King enters the church where he remains for some days, and the people decorate their houses with green branches and new mats. They dress in their best garments, and the head god is taken from the principal morai, and sent round the island carried by the priests. Any persons coming between the god and the sea are immediately stripped of their garments, and the same is done if they do not strip as the god is passing, and lie flat on their faces. This is the season for dancing, boxing, feasting, and all kinds of amusement. When the god arrives from the place whence he first started, the Taboo is taken off. They are generally about thirty days going round, calling at all the villages and plantations, to remind the people that it is time to bring in their taxes, which they do twice a year. This feast ended while I was here on the 24th of December. I have frequently questioned the chiefs about their religion, and their general answer was, that they go to the morais more to feast than pray, which I believe to be really the case. Mr. Cox, or Teymotoo (Keeaumoku), that I have before mentioned, sets the wooden gods and priests at defiance; he says, that they are all liars, and that the white men's God is the true and only God. The Sandwich Islanders have entirely abolished human sacrifices; all the time I have been about these islands, I have not known a single instance of sacrificing a human being.

CHAPTER XIII.

Account of the Customs in the Sandwich Islands continued.

THE natives of the Sandwich Islands are very superstitious; they believe that the spirits of the departed are permitted to revisit this world; and also, that the burning mountain on Owhyhee is hell, and that all wicked people will go there after this life; on the contrary, that those people who are good in this world are made spirits, and permitted to rove about at pleasure. Tameameah is high priest as well as king. When he comes on board a ship he is attended by several chiefs and hikanees, or counsellors, one of whom carries his spit-box; this is considered a very great honour! He is also followed by a sword-bearer, and a file of men with muskets, and a number of attendants with bunches of feathers to keep the flies off, and fans to cool him. His four wives generally accompany him on board. The King never spits any where but in the box, the contents of which, together with grosser evacuations, are taken to sea with his cast-off garments, and committed to the deep; it being his firm belief, that if any person got a part of either, they would have the power to pray him to death. While I remained here I saw many instances of this strange practice. The common people think that it is in the power of the chief priests to pray them to death at pleasure. When on shore I had a small shaving pot and a carving knife stolen; I went to a priest, made him a present of a file, and told him what I had lost, upon which he came to the house, and sent a cryer round the village, proclaiming, that if the articles stolen were not produced before night, all the parties concerned in the theft should be prayed to death. Next morning we found the knife and pot outside of the eating-house door; and I never again lost any thing while I remained on the island. This plan of terrifying these purloiners is an excellent one to prevent theft, and in fact to govern them, as superstition prevails so strongly among them, as to be the only basis on which to build certain laws. The chiefs make use of a root, called *ava*, which is preparing by chewing it well and spitting it into a calabash; and, when they have a sufficient quantity collected, they strainit through the fibres of the cocoa-nut. It is taken daily in small quantities for about a month, and has the effect of intoxicating. When a man first commences taking it, he begins to break out in scales about the head, and it makes the eyes very sore and red, then the neck and breasts. working downwards, till it approaches the feet, when the dose is reduced. At this time the body is covered all over with a white *scruff*, or scale, resembling the dry scurvy. These scales drop off in the order of their formation, from the head, face, neck, and body, and finally leave a beautiful, smooth, clear skin, and the frame clear of all disease:—The process is also held to be a certain cure for venereal infection. I have known many white men go through a course of this powerful medicine. Women are not allowed to use it; and thus, unhappily, the dreadful disease, first brought to these islands by Captain Cook's crew, remains to curse the inhabitants.

The principal employment of the men is tilling the ground, making canoes, spears, etc. The chiefs keep as many followers about them as they can feed and clothe, and when provisions fail with one master, these seek another who is better able to support them. Some are so much attached to their chiefs, that they go off in ships to the N. W. coast of America, and often to China, and, when they return, give all they have earned to their chief, for which he gives them a farm, and they become great men. The old women are employed in making cloth, which is done in the following manner:—they collect a quantity of the bark of the young mulberry-trees, (which are cultivated for that purpose;) they lay it in soak for several days, and then beat it upon a block, which is grooved, or fluted; the stick with which they beat it is also grooved. They beat some as fine as paper, and in this manner they can produce any size, some coarse, and some fine; some they make to stand the water; those are painted in oil colours. The young women rove about without restraint till they attain the age of twenty. They then become more steady and have children. The boys are always practising throwing the spear, swimming, diving, and playing in the surf; flying kites is a favourite amusement; while on shore here I made several. The natives are very great gamblers; their original game is draughts, but instead of having twelve men each, they have about forty; the board is painted in squares, with black and white stones for men, and the game is decided by one party losing all his pieces. They play another game, by hiding a stone under three pieces of cloth. Six people play at this game, each party having his stone and cloths, and a small wand with which they strike the cloth under which they think the stone is deposited. If they do not guess right the first, time the stone is shifted, and so on alternately. I have seen the chiefs sit for a whole day before they decided one game. They are fond of cards, and play whist, all-fours, and *nosey*, extremely well, They often gamble away houses, lands, canoes, and even the clothes off their backs. They are prone to the use of spirituous liquors, and think nothing of taking a tumbler of strong Jamaica rum at a draught. The chief women are, if possible, the greatest drunkards. They distill an excellent spirit from the *tee* root. which grows wild about the mountains, and resembles the beet root of this country. It is, however, larger and much sweeter, of a brownish appearance, and in perfection all the year round. The natives collect a quantity of this root, and bake it well under ground; when sufficiently

baked, they pound it up in an old canoe kept for
that purpose, mixing water with it, and leaving it
to ferment for several days. Their stills are
formed out of iron pots, which they procure
from ships that call here.—These they can enlarge
to any size, by fixing calabashes, or gourds, with
the bottom cut off and made to fit close on the pot,
cemented well with a sort of clay, called *paroro*
(palolo). A copper cone is also affixed, with
which an old gun-barrel is connected, and goes
through a calabash of cold water, which cools
the spirit. The stills are commonly placed by a
stream of water, and they continue to take the
warm water out of the cooler and put in cold; by
which simple process a spirit is produced, not
unlike whiskey, only not so strong, and much
more pleasant. It is called by the natives Y-wer'a
(wai wela), which signifies warm-water, or luma,
trying to imitate the word rum. A man, by the
name of Wm. Stephenson, was the first who
introduced distilling; he was a convict who had
escaped from New South Wales, and lived on
the islands for many years. He has left a large
family behind him. John Young claims the right
of first discovering this mode of distilling; but, in
my opinion, neither of them deserves great credit
for the introduction.

Mr. Manning (Don Marin), a Spaniard, who left
Nootka Sound, on the N. W. coast of America, at
the time the Spaniards formed an establishment
at that place, has cultivated the grape and peach
here. From the former, he makes very good
wine, and, from the latter, good peach brandy,

In company with this man, I went round the island, and found all the plains and valleys in the highest state of cultivation. Tarrow, which is the principal vegetable, grows in abundance; there are two sorts; the first and best is planted in large square patches, banked up about six feet, and beat down very hard at the bottom and sides, so as to hold water; the growers then put a quantity of loose mould, turn some water on, and plant the tarrow in straight lines, or circles; and the water forms a fish pond as well as tarrow patch. This root takes about nine months to come to perfection, They manage it so as to have the patch always full, for as they dig up that which is ripe, they plant the suckers in its room, and by the time they come to the end of a patch, that which was first planted is ripe, and by this means they are never without it. They turn the water from the mountains, bring it down in streams to the tarrow ground, and take it in rotation to turn it on to the different patches. Round the banks of these patches there are beautiful walks, planted with sugar canes and plaintain trees.

The other sort of a tarrow is planted in dry ground, and takes a year to come to perfection. The sweet potato is planted in the same manner, and is hilled up with earth. They have plenty of what are commonly called Irish potatoes, yams, bread-fruit, melons, (both water and musk,) cabbages, onions, celery, garlick; also very good wheat, rice, Indian corn, and every description of fruit that grows in the West Indies; turnips, cucumbers, radishes, salad, in fact all that is produced in England will grow there. On Owhy-hee they have strawberries, raspberries, cranber-ries, and wild apples, and many other kinds of fruit; they have excellent oranges, lemons, limes, citrons, pine-apples, etc., etc.; they also cultivate the tobacco plant, of which the natives use an immense quantity, as men, women and children smoke a great deal. The cotton and coffee grows here very well. They have plenty of cattle, sheep, goats, hogs, ducks, geese, fowls, etc., and a few horses. The cattle go about wild, and are not allowed to be shot without permission from the King Tameameah. Mr. Manning the Span-iard, keeps a large herd of tame cattle, and makes excellent butter and cheese; he has several Indians to take care of them, and they are penned up regularly. Some of the wild cattle often come in with this herd, and are penned up, but allowed to go out in the morning.

CHAPTER XIV.

Account of the Sandwich Islanders continued.—Female dress; that of the men and chiefs —Curious fishing.—Personal Adventure.—Mode of catching flying fish, etc.—Weather.—Ancient fort and novel fortifications.—Superstitious story, and its effects. —Their food, cooking, etc.

THE women of the Sandwich Islands are well made and handsome; their dress consists of ten sheets of cloth of the country, three feet broad and three yards long, wrapped round their waists and descending to the middle of the leg. The outside sheet is prettily painted, and resembles a piece of printed calico: this part of the dress is called pa'ou (pa'u). Their upper garments are composed of sheets, about three yards square; some are painted, some are dyed black, and others white; these they can reduce at pleasure. A tobacco-pipe is hung, with a small looking-glass, round their necks, and they do not consider themselves dressed without them. They also wear an ivory hook, called palava (palaoa), fastened round the neck with the plaited hair of their friends. Some of the women wear their hair long and tied, others cut it close off, turn it up in front, and lime it till quite white; it then looks like the border of a cap. They are very fond of white shirts and black silk handkerchiefs, and look extremely well in them. The men wear a piece of cloth three yards long and a foot wide; this is passed between the legs and round the loins, and is of the stoutest cloth they make. They also wear a cloth over the shoulders the same as the women. The chiefs, on particular occasions, wear a handsome cloak and helmet of feathers, in which dress their appearance is very imposing. They have very fine mats to put on in wet weather, finely painted and fringed. While I was here I was invited by one of the chiefs to join a fishing party on the flats to the westward of the barbour of Honorora. There were several fires lit the night previous, and, in the morning, the nets were run out and set on the flat. The people collected from all parts of the island: they all strip and start from two points, making a circuit of several miles; both parties meet on the outer edge of the flats, and, forming a circle, they gradually close in, keeping their feet close together to prevent the escape of the fish, the water not being more than knee deep. Each person is provided with a scoop net and a bag net over his shoulder; they are permitted to scoop up what they can and fill their bag; still closing in, when the nets are drawn all round after them. By this method they catch 50 or 60 canoe-loads'. There were not fewer than 6000 people collected at this party, which ended, as all such do, in a fight about the division of the fish. On my return from this expedition I was nearly lost: I embarked in a canoe with Toowyheene (Kuwahine), wife to Keymatoo (Keeaumoku), the king's prime minister, who steered the canoe, and when we came to the reef of the harbor wanted to try her skill in dashing through the surf, which ran very high. We got through several breakers, but she at length let the canoe broach too, by which we were upset and all thrown out. The chief's wife and four of the natives collected round me, while the remainder were employed in getting the canoe from the surf and baling her out. I was in a most perilous situation for about half an hour, being obliged to dive through every surf, attended by the natives and the chief's wife, with whose aid I managed to take my clothes off, which made me swim much lighter. We ultimately got safe into the harbour, but I never could be tempted to run over the breakers again.

Having described an aquatic fishing bout, I will now describe the mode of catching flying fish:—The nets in which they are taken are made of twine, which is spun from a sort of hemp, called by the natives oorana (olona), and very strong. A number of nets are laced together, so as to make one of two or three hundred yards in length; they are about six foot broad, with a large and strong bag in the centre, and these they run out in a straight line, the upper part of which is boated by cork wood, and the lower sunk with stones. They take large branches of trees and lay along the head line, which prevent the fish

from flying over; a large double canoe is placed
at each end of the net, gradually drawing it to a
circle, while a number of other canoes are
employed in the open space, beating the water
and diving to frighten the fish toward the net.
When the double canoes at the ends of the net
meet, they take the net in, gradually contracting
the circle till the fish are forced into the bag.
Sometimes, at a haul of this kind, they will catch
six or eight canoes full, though not without risk,
for fishermen often get black eyes and bruised
faces from the fish flying about, which are the
largest I have ever seen. Albicores, dolphins,
and bonitos, are caught in the following manner:
A canoe that pulls seven paddles goes to sea with
two good fishermen, (besides the paddlers), each
with a stout bamboo, about 20 feet long, a strong
line made from the oorana, and about the size of
a log-line, is affixed; the line is about three-quar-
ters of the length of the pole, and has a pearl
hook made fast to it. The canoe is then paddled
very swiftly with the hooks towing on the surface
of the water, one at each side, the fishermen holding the rod steady against their thigh, and the
lower end resting in the bottom of the canoe; they
steady the pole with one hand, and, with the
other keep throwing water on the hook, and when
their prey gets hooked, by lifting the pole upright
the fish swings in, and is caught under the left
arm and secured. In this manner they will take
40 or 50 in the course of a few hours. They have
a sort of heath here which the natives pound up,
and with it dive among the rocks, and, in a few

minutes, all the fish within a certain distance, sicken and come to the surface of the water, and are easily taken. The natives immediately gut them. Whether the fish eat this heath or not I could never learn, but certainly it is a most powerful poison.

On moon light nights, the natives collect on the plain to the number of many hundreds, men, women, and children; here they sit in a ring, where they dance, sing, and play all manner of games, and seldom break up before midnight. On these islands they have much rain in the months of November, December, January, and February, and sometimes it blows heavy gales, equal to the West India hurricanes, from the S.W. These commonly prevail in January, and, during the remainder of the year, the trade-wind blows steady from N. to N. E. sometimes very strong. The hard gales from the S. W. the natives call momotoo (mumuku); previous to the gale, the sea sets in heavily from the S. W. with dark gloomy weather, the mountains are covered with dense clouds, and the tempest is preceded by a dead calm for one or two days, during which time the canoes are not allowed to go on the water. The gale very often blows down the houses, tears tree up by the roots, and does much mischief by overflowing the fish-ponds at the water side, by which means the fish escape. At Woahoo the tide flows 30 minutes past four, full and change, rising about seven feet.

In my tour with Mr. Manning (Manini), we visited the ruin of a large stone house, or fort, which had formerly belonged to a great chief; it had a double fence of human bones round it; these were the bones of his enemies killed in the war before the islands were visited by Europeans. The bones of this great chief are said to be still in the house; the natives are afraid to go near it, preferring to go a round of five or six miles to passing it. Mr. Manning had an island in Pearl River, as before stated, which we also visited. It is about two miles in circumference, having a large cave in the centre. It is covered with goats, hogs, and rabbits. Only one family resides there, consisting of a man, his wife, and three children, with two servants, all belonging to Mr. Manning. We remained on it two days. One evening after supper the man gave us an account of a singular affair, which occurred to him when he first got charge of the island. He was one night awoke by some person calling him by name, and telling him to attend to what he said; he looked up, and was much terrified on beholding the pale form of the late King Pereoranee (Paleioholani) before him, who told him as he valued his life so must he perform what he enjoined: which was, to go to the cave, where he would find his bones with the bones of several great chiefs; he was to take them from thence and convey them to a place of safety, out of the reach of a chief Tereacoo, (Kaleioku) who would come the next day with a party to search the island for the bones of the king and chiefs, to make points for their arrows to shoot rats with, (they think there is a charm in human bones, and never any other sort).

The next day according to the prediction, the chief came and searched the island; the man told him that as the island and all that was on it belonged to a white man of whom Tameameah was very fond, he ought not to come there to search for bones, when there was so many on the main island. The chief took no notice, but searched and took several bundles of bones with him, though not those of the king and chiefs. Tereacoo departed, and on the ensuing night the deceased king and many chiefs appeared to the man, and thanked him for what he had done, assuring him that the white man would protect him, and that he should one day become a great man. Mr. Manning was as superstitious as the natives, and declared he had heard many instances of a similar nature. Shortly after we went to the sleeping-house where the women were. Mr. Manning went out to walk about; in a few minutes he returned in a terrible fright and perspiration. Seeing him look so wild, I asked him what was the matter; when he got more composed, he told me, very seriously, that as he was walking by the prickly pear-trees, saying his prayers and counting his beads, he saw the Chief Tereacoo, who had died about a month since, walking before him, attended by a number of people dressed in the white cloth of the country. I laughed heartily at this relation, and tried to persuade him it was all imagination; but he still persisted in having seen the spirits. The next morning I went round the island, which seems as though it had been kept for a burial place, for I saw hundreds of bundles of human bones, wrapped carefully up in cloth, and laid in the crevices of the rocks. We then left this spot, and Mr. Manning had the king's bones actually conveyed privately to his own house, where he still keeps them. In our tour we were extremely well treated by the natives, each striving who should be most attentive in bringing us roasted pigs, dogs, and powee (poi). They roast their dogs and pigs in a hole in the ground with heated stones, and rolled in leaves of the plaintain-tree; when cooked in this manner, their food, whether meat or fish, is delicious. They prepare the powee by baking the tarrow under ground in the same way, and when thoroughly baked they beat it up on a large flat stone, mixing water with it till they bring it to the consistency of starch; it is then put into calabashes and will keep for one or two months. This with raw fish is their favorite food, which they eat with their fingers, dipping them into the calabash and sucking the powee off. They have also a dish with a raw fish and some salt and water; they dip the fish into the salt and water, and, sucking it, pass it to the person next to them, and so on, till it goes round the company, consisting sometimes of a dozen persons. They are very fond of sea weed, and eat it with salt; shrimps, crabs, and all small fish they eat raw; dogs are considered a great delicacy, and are much dearer than pigs; a number of Europeans prefer dog to pig, declaring, that it is by far the most delicate. The dogs they eat are fed entirely on roots, and never allowed to touch meat. Every plantation we stopped at we had all that the place afforded; the best houses were prepared for our reception, where clean mats and tapas, or cloth of the country, were laid for us to sleep on, which our servants took with them, being their perquisite. About the end of June we got back to the village of Honorora.

214

CHAPTER XV.

Proceedings of a Patriot Ship; fate of the Mutineers of the Rosa; execution of Mr. Griffiths.—The Author takes the Command of the Brig.—They destroy Monterey.— Other Proceedings in these Seas briefly noticed.—The Author returns home.

IN September the ship *Levant*, Captain Carey, of Boston, arrived at Honorora from the Columbia River, and informed us, that the Establishment belonging to the Northwest Company was to be given up to the Americans. We put the remainder of our wood on board this ship, and by the end of September were nearly ready to leave the islands, when a large ship called the *Argentina* touched at Owhyhee. She mounted forty-four guns, belonging to the Independents of South America, and was commanded by Don Hypolito Bouchard, a Frenchman. They had taken many prizes, but none of any value; the crew was very sickly, scarcely enough out of 260 to work the ship. Captain Bouchard demanded the ship *Santa Rosa* and crew from Tameameah, which was immediately complied with. He forgave the men on a promise that they would behave better in future, and brought both ships down to Woahoo to refit. On their arrival, Captain Bouchard came to our houses, where he spent most

215

of his time, often inviting us on board. He took a particular fancy to me, and asked me to command the *Santa Rosa*; to which I agreed, and in October, 1818, entered on my office. We sailed for Atooi, to take on board some of the *Santa Rosa's* mutineers, who had been left there by the brig, and got four of them, but could not find Mr. Griffiths. The Commodore being determined to shoot him, told Tamooree (Kaumualii), that if the man was not produced he would destroy the fort and set fire to the village. Three days after Griffiths was sent in a prisoner, tried by a court martial, and sentenced to be shot, having but two hours to make his peace with the Almighty. He was brought down to the beach (where the Patriot colours were displayed) blindfolded, and shot by four marines, belonging to the *Argentina*. Many hundred of the natives were collected to witness the execution. The corpse was buried on the beach at high-water-mark; the ships then made sail for Woahoo, for some more of the men who had run away, and found that they had escaped to Mowee; the Commodore being determined not to leave a single mutineer on the islands, proceeded thither in pursuit of them, and on arriving learnt that they had gone to the mountains. Don Hypolito then hired a number of natives to pursue the fugitives, and they were brought on board in three days. They were tried by a court martial, one was sentenced to be shot, the others to get twelve dozen lashes; they were brought on deck, and the former was reprieved, but the other received the punishment, which tore his back in a shocking manner. The ships then made sail for Woahoo, where we took on board a supply of hogs and vegetables and a number of natives; and on the 20th of October we took our final leave of those friendly natives, bound for the coast of California, to cruise against the Spaniards. The ship *Santa Rosa* was American built, about 300 tons burthen; mounting eighteen guns, twelve and eighteen pounders; with a compliment of 100 men, thirty of whom were Sandwich Islanders, the remainder where composed of Americans, Spaniards, Portuguese, Creoles, Negroes, Manila men, Malays, and a few Englishmen. The *Argentina* had 260 men, fifty of whom were Islanders, the remainder a mixed crew, nearly similar to that of the *Santa Rosa*. On our passage towards California we were employed exercising the great guns, and putting the ship in good condition for fighting, frequently reading the articles of war which are very strict, and punish with death almost every act of insubordination.

After getting a supply of eggs, oil, etc. from the Russians, we made sail towards the bay of Monterey. The Commodore ordered me into the bay, and to anchor in a good position for covering the landing, while he would keep his ship under weigh, and send his boats in to assist me. Being well acquainted with the bay I ran in and came too at midnight, under the fort; the Spaniard hailed me frequently to send a boat on shore, which I declined. Before morning they had the battery manned, and seemed quite busy. I got a spring on the cable, and at daylight opened a fire on the fort, which was briskly returned from two batteries. Finding it useless to fire at the batteries, the one being so much above us that our shot had no visible effect, the Commodore came in with his boats, and we landed on Point Pinos, about three miles to the westward of the fort; and before the Spaniards had time to bring their field-pieces to attack us, we were on our march against it. We halted at the foot of the hill where it stood for a few minutes, beat a charge and rushed up, the Sandwich Islanders in front with pikes. The Spaniards mounted their horses and fled; a Sandwich Islander was the first to haul down their colours. We then turned the guns on the town, where they made a stand, and after firing a few rounds, the Commodore sent me with a party to assault the place, while he kept possession of the fort. As we approached the town, the Spaniards again fled, after discharging their field-pieces, and we entered without opposition. It was well stocked with provisions and goods of every description, which we commenced sending on board the *Argentina*. The Sandwich Islanders, who were quite naked when they landed, were soon dressed in the Spanish fashion, and all the sailors were employed in searching the houses for money, and breaking and ruining every thing. We took several Creole prisoners, destroyed all the guns in the fort, etc. We had three of our men killed and three taken; next day a party of horsemen came in sight, to whom the Commodore sent a flag of truce, requiring the governor to give up our people and save the town.

218

Three days were granted to consider this proposal, and on the third day, not receiving an answer, he ordered the town to be fired, after which we took plenty of live stock on board, wood, water, etc., and on the 1st day of December got under weigh from Monterey, and stood along the coast to the southward.

On the 4th we made a village, called the Ranch (near Point Conception) where we intended to call for provisions, got the boats all ready, landed a party without opposition, and took the town, all the inhabitants flying on our approach. The men remained all night, and next morning the place was plundered. About noon a lieutenant and two seamen having strayed a short distance from the town, a party of horsemen rushed on them, threw the la's-aws (lasso's) over their heads and dragged them up a neighboring hill, before we could render them any assistance. This so enraged Captain Bouchard, that he ordered the village to be fired instantly, and embarked all the men. After dark we again landed a party well armed to try and surprise the Spaniards and make some prisoners, but they next morning embarked without success. We then weighed and made sail along shore to the southward, two miles from shore, a great number of Spanish troops riding along the beach at whom we fired several shot. In the evening of the 8th of December, we were off the town and mission of St. Barbara, in latitude 34° 36' N. and longitude 119° W.; it falling calm we hoisted the boats out to tow the ships into the bay, where we anchored, the town bearing

N. by W. one mile, seemingly deserted. We fired a gun and hoisted the colours with a flag of truce, and sent a boat on shore to say if they would give up our men we would spare the town; to which the governor agreed, and accordingly on the 10th we got our companions on board, weighed the anchor and made sail to the southward. We again ran into a snug bay, in latitude 33° 33' N., where we anchored under the flag of truce. The bay is well sheltered, with a most beautiful town and mission, about two leagues from the beach. The Commodore sent his boat on shore, to say if they would give us an immediate supply of provisions we would spare their town; to which they replied, that we might land if we pleased, and they would give us an immediate supply of powder and shot. The Commodore was very much incensed at this answer, and assembled all the officers, to know what was best to be done, as the town was too far from the beach to derive any benefit from it. It was, therefore, agreed to land, and give it up to be pillaged and sacked.

Next morning, before daylight, the Commodore ordered me to land and bring him a sample of the powder and shot, which I accordingly did, with a party of 140 men, well armed, with two field-pieces. On our landing, a party of horsemen came down and fired a few shot at us, and ran towards the town. They made no stand, and we soon occupied the place. After breakfast the people commenced plundering; we found the town well stocked with every thing but money and destroyed much wine and spirits, and all the public property; set fire to the king's stores, barracks, and governor's house, and about two o'clock we marched back, though not in the order we went, many of the men being intoxicated, and some were so much so, that we had to lash them on the field-pieces and drag them to the beach, where, about six o'clock, we arrived with the loss of six men. Next morning we punished about twenty men for getting drunk.

On the 23rd of December we saw the island of Ceres, and hauled up for the east end of the island; in the afternoon we were boarded by some Russian hunters in bodarkees, assisted by about twenty of which we, at daylight, hoisted the boats out and towed to the anchorage. We came too on the S. E. side of the island, three quarters of a mile from the village: the Russians were landed here by an American brig for the purpose of hunting the sea otter, on this as well as on the other islands about this coast. Their village consisted of about twenty miserable huts, covered with the skins of the sea lion and elephant, which are very plentiful. English and American ships frequently call here to fill up their oil.

We had a party on shore daily hunting the deer, which are the only animals on the island, and killing the sea lion and elephant for the sake of their hearts and tongues, which we found very good. While we lay here five of the former mutineeers took the first whale boat in the night and ran away. We sent the launch in pursuit of them, but it returned in three days, without having seen them.   Captain Bouchard swore if he caught them he would immediately shoot them.

January 18th, 1819, having completed our wood and water, and refitting the ships, we got under weigh, intending to cruise off St. Blas, for the Manila ships.

January 22nd, we saw Cape St. Lucas, E. by S. about 30 miles, the sea all round was covered with turtles, which we took on board as we wanted them.   On the 24th, captured and scuttled a merchant brig.

We sent a party on shore at the Tres Marias to wood and water.   We found a root resembling the tarrow of the Sandwich Islands; the Islanders cooked some of it in the island fashion, and immediately after they had eaten of it their bodies and faces became swelled and bloated in a terrible manner, some died in a few days, and others lingered for ten days in the greatest agony.   The Commodore lost twelve men in his manner.   The Tres Marias are covered with wood, chiefly lignum-vitæ, black and white ebony, hard cedar, and many other kinds.   There are plenty of parrots, monkeys, snakes, guanas, pigeons, doves, etc., and abundance of fish.   We continually kept a party on shore hunting and fishing; in digging for fresh water we found plenty of ore, which our prisoners said was silver; the water is very bad, and brackish.

On the 9th, of July we made the harbour of Valparaiso.   His Majesty's ships *Andromache* and *Icarus* were here, with all Lord Cochrane's squadron fitting out for Lima.   On the 17th, the

Argentina arrived in very great distress for provisions and water; she had buried about forty men; the ships were laid up, and most ot the crews entered on board the Chilian fleet.

I now applied to Captain Bouchard for my pay and prize-money, and told him I was heartily sick of the service of the Independents, and that I intended to go to England in the first vessel that sailed for that country, the port being then embargoed on account of the expedition going against Peru; he replied that he could not pay me, unless I continued in the service and took the ship to Buenos Ayres; which I declined doing, and left her in charge of Mr. Woodburn, the first Lieutenant.

Lord Cochrane's squadron were wretchedly manned; they send parties of soldiers up the country and impress the countrymen and send them on board the fleet; half the complement of each ship is composed of Chileno's and blacks; their troops are chiefly black.

We do not find sufficient interest in the sequel of these adventures to render it advisable to give the details, and shall only add, that the writer of this journal, Mr. Corney, arrived in London on the 15th, of February, 1820, after an absence of nearly seven years, full of vicissitudes.

APPENDIX.

Note:—In the year 1847, Mr. R. C. Wyllie, who was for many years, the Hawaiian Minister of Foreign Affairs, discovered a number of letters and other documents, belonging to the estate of the late Don Francisco de Paula y Marin, in a house in the old fort.

Most of them were filed in the Government archives, and are still in existence, although unfortunately Don Marin's diary has been lost. Among them are the following letters from Capt. Bouchard of the frigate "Argentina," addressed to Don Juan de Elliot y Castro and Don Marin, as well as his instructions from the Provisional government of Buenos Ayres.

THE BOUCHARD LETTERS.

(TRANSLATION.)

I. The Sovereign Congress of the United Provinces of Rio de La Plata.

Information having reached this Government of the scandalous conduct of the crew of the corvette called "Santa Rosa," Don Hipolito de Bouchard, sergeant major of the navy of this state, and commander of the war frigate "Argentina," has been duly authorized and invested with power to proceed over the same route hitherto cruised by said vessel, and wherever the said ship may be found with all belonging to it, to seize it or reclaim it from any government, as also any member of the crew. We request any government or state, in such case, to deliver it up to said commander; that all the effects of said vessel be delivered with the

224

armament, ammunition and stores belonging to it; to which we sign and seal with the coat of arms of this state, 27th, of April 1818.

> DR. FRANCISCO SANS, President.
> JUAN JOSE PASO. Vocal.
> DR. DON PEDRO ELIAS, Secretary,
> (and seven others).

II.   I have just received at this date the excellent order of His Majesty in which he states the following:— That H. M. has been pleased to order that the pilot deliver to me every thing belonging to the corvette "Santa Rosa," and at the same time that he deliver to the bearer six barrels for vegetables, * * * the consumption said men * * * * * *

For the compliment in which I most heartily thank His Majesty, as I do you, for the unbounded kindness you have manifested in providing for the ships belonging to the United Provinces of Rio de La Plata.

I communicate to you how we are situated here, in the same state as before your departure, (for I have been in your confidence), which would not permit our coming to Kavacacao (Kawaiakekua?) for you must be aware of the great loss to my expedition, and the great consumption of provisions and water, without the slightest remuneration, but withal sustaining a great loss.

The individual to whom His Majesty has been pleased to assign the delivery of the sweet potatoes, not having received the barrels, which were all in use, was given a basket which measured the same quantity, in order that he might deliver what had been ordered, but has refused to receive it, and says that he will return thus from Kayroa; all of which I communicate to you for your information.

May God preserve you many years.

"Argentina," 30th Aug., 1818.

HIPOLITO BOUCHARD.

SR. DON DE ELIOT Y CASTRO.

Sec. of H. M.

III.   Because of the difficulties which may arise in regard to the vessels belonging to the United Provinces of Rio de La Plata, e. g. mutinies, escapes, etc, as happened formerly in the case of the corvette "Santa Rosa," I authorize in the name of the nation of the United Provinces of Rio de La Plata, King Kamehameha to proceed as follows with any ship taking refuge within his dominions:—to hold the vessel with all its effects and crew, to deprive them of all means of communication, to take down the testimony of all the crew, examining its papers which should contain the number of the patents; taking note of the number of men comprising the crew, as also of its orders and its private instructions; for in these will be found whether the vessel has been duly commissioned: should it not possess these documents, and should it be armed for war, or have plunder on board, it will be suspicious, and must be held with all its effects and crew until due notice be given to the Government; observing to regard and care for said vessel until the resolution taken by the Government of Buenos Ayres near (por) the coasts of Chili (be received.)

His Majesty Tameamea (Kamehameha) is requested to observe the utmost punctuality and order in these cases.   This authority being given by Senor Don Hipo-

lito Bouchard, Commander of the frigate "Argentina,
6th, of Sept., 1818.

HIPOLITO BOUCHARD.

Senor Don Francisco de Paula y Marin.

IV.   Dear Sir:—

I have had the misfortune not to find the brig-
antine of which I was in search, and have found only
four of the seamen, among them the chief of the
mutiny from aboard the "Santa Rosa;" who, for his
crime has gone to give account to the Almighty.   I
have aboard a sailor who had come from Oahu with
Capt. Cary.   I request you on receipt of this letter, if
the men who escaped have been found, to send them
to me immediately, as also some provisions, as potatoes,
taros, and pork.   You will kindly make out the full
account in order that it may be settled; for it seems to
me that I have not paid for the three casks of sweet
potatoes which I have received from you, and for
which I will settle on my arrival.   I send you the cask
which you loaned me for measuring the brandy, and
about which I had forgotten.

Remember me to Captain Ebbitt and to Capt. Davis;
have the kindness to give my best wishes to Governor
Boki, and ask him to send me six pieces of timber for
(canones?), the same as those of which I spoke to you
before my departure; and should he deliver them, send
the bill that I may settle it: all of which I shall esteem
a favor from you as well as from the Governor; also
send some hogs, if they can be obtained.

May God keep you many and happy years.

"Argentina," 8th October, 1818.

HIPOLITO BOUCHARD.

Senor Don Francisco de Paula y Marin.

V. My dear Sir:—

My present need compels me to trouble you for your attention to matters which no one can settle better than you; owing to your acquaintance with these places, and your proficiency in the language.

My friend, it appears that the King and his Secretary have taken advantage of the kindness of Mr.—— an honorable man, in regard to the wood which he has given me in payment for 44 bales of fine goods and six bolts of silks. It appears that the American Captains do not wish to take the sandal wood which his Majesty has given me in payment for said goods, and I find myself compelled to appeal to the Governor, so that through your intercession be made clear the bargain for the sandal-wood, which the American Captains will not accept: he (Governor) may take the matter in hand and give you, from the lot belonging to the King, the quantity to replace that which was not genuine; this affair troubles me daily, and I cannot wait longer than day after tomorrow, and you may see the best way to settle it.

You must be aware that two armed ships, containing their crews of 290 men, are very expensive, and cost upwards of $150 daily; so if the King has deceived him (Mr.——) giving me fire-wood instead of sandal-wood, charging me $10.00 a picul, I shall in consequence charge him with all the expenses of my vessels during the time this business detains me, and hold the King responsible for them.

I request you as a man who understands these matters, to interview the Governor, making clear to him the cause of my complaints, and have him immediately replace the sandal-wood which was not genuine, delivering it to the Captain of the Frigate "Sultana,"

Mr. Caleb Reynolds, which is all I have to request of the Governor at present.

May God keep you many and happy years.

"Argentina," Sept. 2nd, 1818.

HIPOLITO BOUCHARD.

There is another letter in the collection, from Capt. Bouchard to Don Marin, dated Dec. 20, 1819 at Valparaiso, inquiring about a brig, the crew of which were supposed to have run away with it.

THE BOUCHARD LETTERS.
(ORIGINALS.)

I. El Soberano Congreso De Las Provincias Unidas Del Rio De La Plata.

Habiendo llegado á noticia á esta soberania el escandaloso exceso de la tripulacion de la corveta nombrada Santa Rosa, se ha expedido poder al sarjento mayor de la marina de este Estado, y comandante de la fragata Argentina de guerra, Don Hipolito de Buchard: y para que corra por donde dicha corveta cruzaba: y para que con todo en cualesquiera destino que sea hallado este buque queda apresarlo ó reclamarlo d cualquiera Gobierno, y en seguida cualesqniera individuo de su tripulacion. Se suplica, á cualquiera gobierno ó estado, se digne, en tal caso, exederlo á dicho comandante. Se exedan todos los intereses de dicho buque, armamento, municion y armamento que corres' pondan. Para lo cual lo firmamos y sellamos con las armas de este Estado á 27 del mes de Abril del año de mil ochocientos diez y ocho.

Dr. Francisco Sans, Presidente.

Juan Jose Paso, Vocal.

Dr. Don Pedro Elias, Segretario.

(and seven others).

II.   Con esta fecha acabo de recibir la superior orden de su Magestad donde il me expone lo siguiente; que Su Magestad se ha dignado ordenar al piloto que se me entrege todo aquello que fuese perteneciente á la corveta Santa Rosa, y al mismo tiempo, que al portador se le entrege seis barriles para los vegetales, consumo que dicho hombre   *   *   *   *

Para su complimiento en lo que doy infinitas gracias á Su Magestad y á Usted por consiguente por la immensa bondad que Usted usa para el auxilio de los buques de las Provincias Unidas del Rio de la Plata. Comunico á Umd. como estamos aqui en el mismo ser que antes de irse Usted pues yo he estado en la confianza de Usted, no dejaria de venir á esta Kawacacao (Kawaiakekua), pues no debe Usted ignorar el atraso de mi expedition, el gran consumo de viveres, y aguada sin la menor utilidad, si no con todo un gran atraso.

El individuo que Su Magestad se ha dignado destinar para entregar las batatas, no habiendo podido absolutamente dar se le los barriles por tenerlos todos ocupados, se le dió una canasta que podia hacer la misma cuantidad para que por el entregara lo que se habia ordenado, el que no ha querido recibir y me dice que se vuelve si de Kayroa.

Lo cual comunico á Usted para su inteligencia.

Dios guarde á Usted muchos años. "Argentina," 30 de Agosto de 1313.   Hipolito Bouchard.

Señor Don Juan de Eliot y Castro,
                Secretario de Su Magestad.

III.   Por los inconvenientes que pueden suceder, respeto á los buques de las Provincias Unidas del Rio de la Plata, e. g. fugas, levantamientos, al caso sucedido anteriormente con la Corveta Santa Rosa, doy facultad, en nombre de la Nacion de las Provincias Unidas del Rio de la Plata, al Rey Tameamea (Kamehameha), que cualesquiera buque que se refugiase bajo su dominio tome las providencias siguientes; de tener el buque con todo sus intereses y la gente, ponerlas en-comunicables, informa una sumaria y tomando las declaraciones de toda la tripulacion, y visitando sus papeles que deben contener o el numero de las paten-tes; notando en ellas la cuantidad de hombres que contiene la tripulacion; se pase ordenanza y sus in-struciones secretas, que en ellas se conocerá si el buque está despedido en orden, y si acaso no tuviese estos documentos el buque será sospechoso si fuere armado en guerra y si fuese cualesquiera presa deten-gase el buque sus intereses y su tripulacion hasta la parte, al Gobierno, con el bien entendido respectar y cuidar los intereses que en dicho buque se refugiasen en estos dominios, hasta la resolucion del Gobierno de B. Ayres por las costas de Chile. Se suplica á su Magestad Tameamea la mayor puntualidad y orden en estos casos. Dado este poder por el Señor Don Hipo-lito Bouchard, Comandante de la Fragata Argentina á 6 dias del mes de Setiembre de 1818.

Hipaulito Bouchard.

Señor Don Francisco de Paula y Marin.

IV. Muy Senor mio: he tenido la desgracia de no encontrar el bergantin que iba á buscar, y solamente he encontrado cuatro de los marineros de dicho buque, y entre ellos al cabeza principal del motin, de abordo de la Santa Rosa, el cual por su delito ha ido á dar cuenta al todo poderoso, y un marinero que habia venido de Waooh (Oahu), con el Capitan Kery (Cary), lo tengo abordo. Suplico á Usted que al recibir esta si se hallan los tales hombres que fugaron, me los empresta en el momento, y lo mismo con algunas provisiones, como batatas, taros y chancho. Y Vm. formerá la cuenta de todo para satisfacer su importe lo mismo: que me parece no he pagado las tres barricas de batatas que he tomado de Vmd, que sa satisfacere á mi llegada, Remito al Vmd. la barrica que Vmd, me empresto para medir e, aguardiente que se me habia olvidado. Expresiones al Capitan Eviet (Ebbitt) y al Capitan Devis (Davis), de mi parte. Tenga Nmd, la molestia de dar muchas memorias al Gobernador M. Poquit (Boki) y suplicarle Vmd, de mi parte que me mande seis piezas de madera para canones como habia hablado á Vmd antes de mi salida, y si acaso los libra, mandeme Vmd la cuenta para satisfacer su importe, que mereceré de Vmd y del Gobernador lo mismo. Y algunos chanchos si se pueden consequir en el momento. Dios guarde á Vmd muchos y felices años.

Hipaulito Bouchard.

"Argentina." 8 de Octubre de 1818.

Señor Don Francisco de Paula y Marin.

V. M. S. M. la necesidad en que me hallo me obliga á molestar la atencion de Vmd. sobre cosas que nadie mas que Vmd puede hacer transar (transigir)? nuestras dificultades por el gran conocimiento que Vmd tiene en estos lugares, y la perfeccion que Vmd tiene para el idioma. Amigo, parece que el Rey y su secretario han engañado la bondad de—hombre de bien, sobre el palo que me ha dado en pago de 44 fardos de generos finos y seis bultes de sederias.

Segun parece los SS Capitanes Americanos no quieren tomar el sangilut que Su Magestad me ha dado en pago de dichos efectos, y yo me veo precisado de Oluxxia al S. Gobernador para que con la persona de Vmd le haga entender el trato del sangilut, que no quieren tomar los Americanos, él se puede hacer cargo, y darle la cantidad que fuese mala de la que pertence al Rey: para mi todos los dias me es un daño terrible, y no puedo detenerme mas que hasta pasado mañana, y Vmd. vea el mejor modo para este. Vmd. no ignora que con dos buques armad s que contienen sus tripulaciones de 290 hombres, los gastos son de una gran consideracion, y suben á mas de ciente cinquenta pesos diarios, y si el Reyé ha engañado su buena fé, dandome leña de quemar por sanguilut, cargandome a diez pesos el pico en consequencia de esto, todos los dias que me detenge este negocio, cargaré los gastos que hago abordo de mis dos buques, para que el Rey me sea responsable de ellos.

Suplico la bondad de Vmd. como hombre que entiende estos negocios, se aproxime al Gobernador, haciendo entender mis quejas y que determine en la hora misma de remplagar el sangilut que no fuese bueno, entregandolo al Capitan de la Fragata Sultano, Don Caleb Reynolds, que es la unica cosa que suplicaré la éd bondad del Señor Gobernador y en este caso. Dios guarde á Vmd muchos y felices años.

Hipaulito Bouchard.

"Argentina," Setiembre 2 de 1818.

INDEX.

INDEX.

INDEX.

236

NAVIGATIO